W

THE

ULTIMATE

HOLLYWOOD

TOUR BOOK

To Adele

THE ULTIMATE

HOLLYWOOD

TOUR BOOK

THE INCOMPARABLE GUIDE TO MOVIE STARS' HOMES, MOVIE AND TV LOCATIONS, SCANDALS, MURDERS, SUICIDES, AND ALL THE FAMOUS TOURIST SITES

WILLIAM A. GORDON

NORTH RIDGE BOOKS
Lake Forest, CA

W

OTHER BOOKS BY WILLIAM A. GORDON

SHOT ON THIS SITE
A Traveler's Guide to the Places and Locations Used to
Film Famous Movies and Television Shows

FOUR DEAD IN OHIO
Was There a Conspiracy at Kent State?

THE QUOTABLE WRITER
Words of Wisdom from Mark Twain, Aristotle, Oscar
Wilde, Robert Frost, Erica Jong, and More

A NOTE TO OUR READERS

Even the best tour guides need to be periodically updated, and *The Ultimate Hollywood Tour Book* is no exception. That is why we offer to e-mail updates to our readers. We can let you know almost instantly if we discover a new movie location or if a celebrity sells his or her property or if a museum, restaurant, or tour opens or closes.

To receive our "List of Updates," all you have to do is e-mail us at info@nrbooks.com and tell us which edition you are reading. (Just look at the next page for the copyright date.) And if you send us a tip that we can use, we will send you a free copy of the next edition of this book.

Tour groups interested in special sales, promotions, or in creating customized tours may contact us at the above address or e-mail us at info@nrbooks.com.

Fourth Edition
22

Library of Congress Cataloging-in-Publication Data
   Gordon, William A.
   The ultimate Hollywood tour book: the incomparable guide to
movie stars' homes, movie and TV locations, scandals, murders,
suicides, and all the famous tourist sites / William A. Gordon—Third
Ed.
      p. cm.
   ISBN 978-0937813-08-9
   1. Motion picture actors and actresses—Homes and haunts—
California—Los Angeles—Guidebooks. 2. Motion picture locations—
California—Los Angeles—Guidebooks.
   3. Hollywood (Los Angeles, Calif.)—Guidebooks. 4. Motion picture
actors and actresses—Biography—Miscellanea.
   5. Hollywood (Los Angeles, Calif.)-Social life and customs.
   I. Title
   PN 1993.5.U65G635 1992
   791.43'09794'940904 9—dc20

ISBN 978-0937813-08-9
LCCO 2007920156

CONTENTS

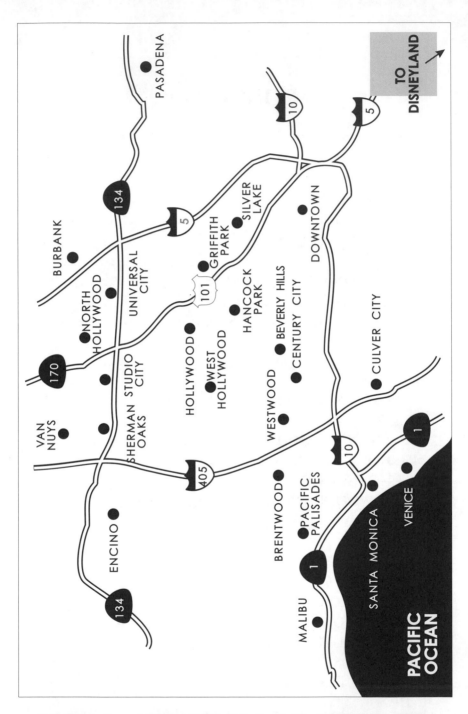

MAP 1   GREATER LOS ANGELES

INTRODUCTION

The Ultimate Hollywood Tour Book was written for the millions of people who visit Southern California each year and who, not knowing how to find the real attractions of Tinseltown, take prepackaged bus tours to celebrities' homes or go on studio tours that show them only what the studios want the public to see.

This book will take you to places you will not be shown on any organized tour. We will show you where the major stars of both today and yesteryear live (or have lived—stars such as Madonna, Elvis Presley, Marilyn Monroe, Arnold Schwarzenegger, Britney Spears, and Tom Cruise.

The Ultimate Hollywood Tour Book will show you where you have the best chances of actually seeing the stars. Although it is always fun to see where they live, you probably will not see them outside their gated mansions and homes. However, there is a good chance you will see someone famous if you go to one of the restaurants, hotels, or hot spots that attract a celebrity clientele. Dozens of such establishments are profiled in this book.

We will show you where, throughout greater Los Angeles, dozens of classic or highly popular motion pictures have been filmed—movies such as *E.T., Pretty Woman, Collateral, Independence Day, Speed, The Nutty Professor, The 40-Year-Old Virgin, The Italian Job, Die Hard, The Terminator* (and its sequels), the *Back to the*

Future series, the *Beverly Hills Cop* series, *Chinatown,* and *Father of the Bride.*

We will show you how to find famous locations such as the "L.A. Law" building," The Bat Cave, the "My Name is Earl" hotel, and the houses or apartments seen in popular television shows: "Desperate Housewives," "Alias," "Melrose Place," "Dynasty," "The Brady Bunch," "Seinfeld," "Malcolm in the Middle," and "Beverly Hills 90210."

We will show you where some of Hollywood's most notorious murders, suicides, and scandals have occurred. You will see where O. J. Simpson allegedly murdered his ex-wife Nicole and her friend Ron Goldman; where the Manson clan struck (in a home Candice Bergen lived in just a few months earlier); where Marilyn Monroe, John Belushi, Janis Joplin, and River Phoenix fatally overdosed; and where the Menendez brothers gunned down their parents in cold blood.

We will take you to other locations that may surprise you. How many of you know, for example, that John Dean, the man who brought down Richard Nixon's presidency, now lives in Beverly Hills? Or that Nixon himself lived in Brentwood and Beverly Hills after losing the 1960 election? Would you like to see where John F. Kennedy's most notorious mistress lived? Or where Ronald Reagan lived when he was elected president—or his retirement home? Virtually all of Reagan's Los Angeles area residences can be found in this book.

We will also show you how to find the major studios and world-famous attractions such as Grauman's Chinese Theater and the popular Universal Studios tour.

The focus of this book, of course, is not on the commercial attractions or the usual tourist traps. The tours and the television ticket outlets are included because one cannot write a guide book about Hollywood and not mention them.

The emphasis in this book is on the hidden or unpublicized attractions—the ones that Hollywood insiders know about, but which tourists usually never know exist.

This book is arranged geographically and starts with a self-guided tour of the celebrities' homes in the so-called Platinum Triangle: Beverly Hills, Bel-Air, and the lesser known but actually more expensive residential area of Holmby Hills.

Maps to these celebrities' homes are hawked on seemingly every street corner along Sunset Boulevard and in every souvenir shop in town. However, the tour presented in this book is very different from what those maps offer. For one, the maps in this book are up to date (and are updated in each edition). More importantly, the addresses have been verified through searches of public records.

In addition, *The Ultimate Hollywood Tour Book* is the first Hollywood tour book to not only show where the major celebrities of the past and present live (or have lived) but also to tell something about the history of these homes.

(Incidentally, the people who sell the maps to the stars' homes would have you believe that most motion picture and television stars live in Beverly Hills and Bel-Air. Actually, only a small percentage of the best-known living actors live on the streets covered by such maps. As this book shows, celebrities live all over greater Los Angeles. Observant readers will also note that the younger stars tend to live in the Hollywood Hills and outlying areas. Very few celebrities under the age of 40 live in Beverly Hills.)

Subsequent chapters highlight celebrities' homes,

movie locations, historic entertainment industry sites, and other points of interest in Brentwood, Pacific Palisades, Malibu, Venice and Santa Monica, Culver City, Westwood and Century City, the Sunset Strip, West Hollywood, Fairfax and the Miracle Mile, Hancock Park and the Wilshire District, downtown Los Angeles, the Hollywood Hills, Pasadena, the San Fernando Valley, and, of course, Hollywood itself.

Although the tours presented here very roughly circle the city, the author realizes that tourists will start from many different points of town and will, instead of following any sequence presented, tour the areas that are either closest to them or of most interest to them.

To make the most of your trip to Los Angeles, I suggest that you read the entire book first, choose the areas of greatest interest and, using the maps provided, combine the tours as you see fit. (For example, tours of the Sunset Strip and Beverly Hills can be very easily combined.)

There is really a great deal to see—and you will find, despite rumors to the contrary, that Los Angeles is one of the greatest places in the world to go sightseeing.

In fact, that is why I live here: because I get to go sightseeing every day.

BEVERLY HILLS, BEL-AIR, AND HOLMBY HILLS

Whenever I show people around Beverly Hills, I like to get behind certain tour buses, tell my passengers what the tour guides are saying, and then let my passengers know who really lives in those homes.

I do not mean to suggest that most of the tours are unreliable or in any way disreputable (although I did hear one person affiliated with one major studio tour joke about "the new lies our guides are making up this week").

I am merely suggesting that the tour guides—usually aspiring actors between gigs—have, on occasion, used their highly creative talents when telling people about who lives where in Beverly Hills.

Tour guides have been known to move celebrities from one street to another—or from one part of town to another—just to spice up the tours.

One might say that they sometimes play a version of celebrity musical chairs so they have something to say while driving on streets where no one particularly notable has ever lived.

Of course, another, probably even more important, reason why the tours of Beverly Hills do not always meet the highest standards of accuracy is that the tours are based on maps to the stars' homes that have been around since at least 1924 (real estate agents used to publish them themselves to lure prospective homebuyers to Beverly Hills). These maps are an inescapable part of life in L.A.

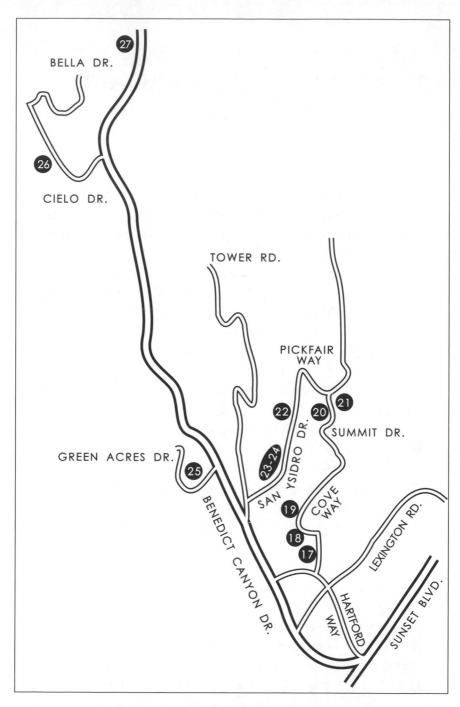

MAP 3   BEVERLY HILLS

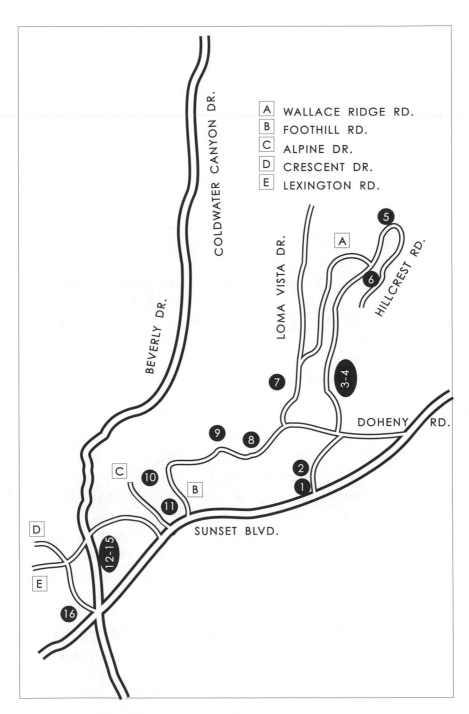

A   WALLACE RIDGE RD.
B   FOOTHILL RD.
C   ALPINE DR.
D   CRESCENT DR.
E   LEXINGTON RD.

COLDWATER CANYON DR.

LOMA VISTA DR.

BEVERLY DR.

HILLCREST RD.

A

DOHENY   RD.

SUNSET BLVD.

MAP 2   BEVERLY HILLS

They are hawked on seemingly every street corner along Sunset Boulevard in Beverly Hills and in virtually every souvenir shop along Hollywood Boulevard.

The best-selling map is called simply "Map of Movie Stars' Homes." Even though celebrities move as often, if not more often, than regular folk, the current edition of the map is remarkably similar to a 1977 edition on file at the Beverly Hills Public Library.

The reason the mapmakers do not keep up with celebrity comings and goings is because they have no incentive to. After all, their customers never know the difference. Tourists who are in town for a short period do not have the time or the inclination to independently verify the information they are given—even if they knew how to.

Of course, a few people in Hollywood like to keep up with the latest celebrity real estate transactions. You are lucky: I happen to be one of them.

The following tour, you can follow in lieu of paying $25 to $30 to go on a bus tour, brings Beverly Hills touring up to date and reflects who lives, or has lived, in the houses in Beverly Hills, Bel-Air, and Holmby Hills, each time at the time we go to press (which is usually once a year).

I have included driving directions to help you get around Beverly Hills, but I have not done so for most other parts of town. Beverly Hills is a special case. Its residential streets twist and turn so much that they often look like pretzels. Not only are the streets sometimes confusing for the uninitiated, but several of them change names in midcourse—and sometimes more than once.

A recent article in the *Los Angeles Times* told the story of typical tourists who found following the existing maps to stars' homes so frustrating that they gave up and went to the beach instead.

The directions that accompany the text and maps

should make your sightseeing a much more enjoyable experience.

Please note: These houses are private residences. You can drive by them, admire them, and be what we call a "lookie-loo," but you should never, ever disturb the privacy of the individuals who live in them.

If you approach a celebrity at his or her home, he or she may construe the approach as a hostile act and respond accordingly.

Remember: not all celebrities are as volatile as Sean Penn or Sean Young. But why take a chance?

While it is always possible that you may see celebrities outside their homes (I've seen Madonna jogging, Ted Danson's kids playing, and Valerie Harper walking her dogs), any such sightings are strictly up to chance. The likelihood is that you will not see celebrities outside their homes.

If you want to see movie stars, go to one of the many restaurants or hotels they frequent. This book lists dozens of establishments where you have a good chance of seeing someone famous.

The following tour can be taken just to get a general sense of how and where celebrities and Los Angeles's upper class live.

(DIRECTIONS: This tour starts at the intersection of Sunset Boulevard and Hillcrest Drive, which is located one mile east of Beverly Hills Hotel and just west of the Sunset Strip. You will be traveling north on Hillcrest Drive.

If you are on Sunset headed east, make a left turn onto Hillcrest Drive. If you are coming from Hollywood or the Sunset Strip and headed west, turn right.)

1-6. CELEBRITY HOUSES ON HILLCREST DRIVE

The first house on the left—which would be on the northwest corner of Sunset and Hillcrest (or 9401 Sunset Boulevard)—was formerly owned by singer Phil Collins.

A few houses up, you will pass the last home of Albert "Cubby" Brocculi, the producer of the first 17 James Bond movies. Brocculi lived at 809 Hillcrest Dr. His estate sold the house in 2005 for close to its $25 million asking price.

At the corner of Doheny Road, you will see the sign welcoming you to Truesdale Estates. There you will find the homes of comedian and character actor Morey Amsterdam, who played Buddy on "The Dick Van Dyke Show" (1012 Hillcrest Drive); and comedian Groucho Marx (1083 Hillcrest Drive).

If you continue north past Wallace Ridge, you can also see, at 1174 Hillcrest, the split-level French-regency style house that Elvis Presley bought in May 1967 shortly after his marriage to Priscilla. Elvis did not live in that house for very long. A few months after buying this house, he decided he wanted to buy a home that afforded more privacy, and moved to 144 Monovale Drive, the last of several homes in which he lived in Los Angeles. That last home, which is featured later in this tour, is probably the more interesting of the two.

Comedian Danny Thomas lived in a mansion he called Villa Roisa at 1187 Hillcrest Drive, which is at the end of the street; and it was there, on May 21, 1980, that his daughter Marlo married talk show host Phil Donahue. The best place to view the Thomas estate, though, is not from up close, but from a distance on Wallace Ridge.

Instead of continuing on Hillcrest, make a left turn onto Wallace Ridge, and stop around 1081 Wallace Ridge, a pink mansion that the rock star Prince once lived in and which tour guides still point out as his. If you look to your left you can see Thomas' home from across the ravine. It is the last home on the right of the mountain.

After viewing Thomas' estate, continue down Wallace Ridge and make a left onto Loma Vista Drive.

7. GREYSTONE MANSION, 905 Loma Vista Drive

This magnificent 55-room mansion, built in 1923, was the largest and most expensive home in Beverly Hills in the 1920s. It was built by oilman Edward Doheny—the same Edward Doheny who was embroiled in the Teapot Dome scandal. Doheny, who was not content with his personal fortune of $100,000,000, was accused of paying President Warren G. Harding's Secretary of the Interior, Albert Fall, a $100,000 bribe in return for secret leases to government oil reserves at Elk Hills and Buena Vista in California. His trial ended in an acquittal.

In 1928 Doheny built the mansion as a gift for his only son, Edward Jr., who moved in with his wife and children. A few weeks later, however, Edward Jr. and his male secretary, Hugh Plunkett, were both found dead in Doheny's bedroom, giving rise to unconfirmed rumors that they died in a lovers' quarrel.

Edward Jr.'s widow continued to live at Greystone until 1955, when Henry Crown, the owner of the Empire State Building, paid $25 million for the estate and subdivided it. What remained of the property was subsequently leased to the American Film Institute, and is now a public park owned and operated by the city of Beverly Hills.

If you stop at Greystone, do not be surprised to see movie crews. The mansion and grounds have frequently been used as a movie location, and the films *Ghostbusters* (where it was used as Gracie Mansion), *Spiderman, Austin*

Powers in Goldmember, All of Me, The Witches of Eastwick, Batman & Robin, The Bodyguard, Indecent Proposal, The Fabulous Baker Boys, Death Becomes Her, and *The Beautician and the Beast* have all filmed here. So have television programs such as "Dynasty," "Falcon Crest," and "Knots Landing."

(DIRECTIONS: After leaving Greystone, make a right turn onto Loma Vista Drive and then another right onto Doheny Drive.)

8. FORMER OZZY AND SHARON OSBOURNE HOME, 513 N. Doheny Drive
    The Osbournes lived in this six-bedroom estate when they filmed their 2002-2005 MTV reality series, "The Osbournes." One British critic, noting how dysfunctional the family was, said that "they have become the biggest hit show in MTV's history means the culture has thoroughly collapsed."

9. FORMER HOME OF TALK SHOW HOST AND BUSINESS EXECUTIVE MERV GRIFFIN, 603 N. Doheny Road (at the corner of Schuyler)
    Griffin's credits include hosting his own talk show and creating "Jeopardy" and "Wheel of Fortune."

(DIRECTIONS: After seeing Merv's former home, continue on Doheny Drive, then make a left turn onto Foothill Road.)

10. FRANK SINATRA'S LAST HOME, 915 Foothill Drive

Frank Sinatra suffered his fatal heart attack at this mansion on May 14, 1998. Former Universal Studios chairman Lew Wasserman lived in the home next door at 911 Foothill Drive.

(DIRECTIONS: Make a right at Sunset Boulevard—at an intersection where Lindsay Lohan was arrested on suspicion of drunk driving—and make a quick right on Alpine Drive.)

11. FORMER HOME OF TOM CRUISE AND KATIE HOLMES, 809 Alpine Drive

Numerous tabloids, TV shows, and maps to stars' homes have identified this gated mansion, just past the intersection of Alpine and Lexington Drives, as the one Tom Cruise leased between 2001 and 2008. The $55,000-a-month house had previously been leased by Eddie Murphy and Elton John.

(DIRECTIONS: Reverse directions and return to Sunset Boulevard, making a right turn onto Sunset.

Continue traveling west for a few blocks until you see the sign that says: "Beverly Drive/Crescent Drive." Make a right onto Beverly Drive)

12-15. HOMES ON BEVERLY DRIVE

From Sunset Boulevard, make a right turn onto Beverly Drive, a street that was once owned in its entirety by Beverly Hills' first mayor, humorist and silent film star Will Rogers. Rogers had a home at 925 N. Beverly until about 1928, when he moved to Pacific Palisades. Singer Pat Boone lived at 904 Beverly Drive. Carolyn Jones, who played Morticia in the television series "The Addams Family," lived at 907 Beverly, and "M*A*S*H" star Wayne Rogers lived at 916 Beverly.

At the corner of Beverly and Lexington Drives, make a left turn onto Lexington Road. And then make another left on Lexington. This will lead you to the Beverly Hills Hotel.).

16. BEVERLY HILLS HOTEL AND BUNGALOWS, 9641 Sunset Boulevard, (310) 276-2251; (800) 283-8885

The Beverly Hills Hotel is one of the most famous hotels in the world. It was built by developer Burton Green in 1912, and it is often said that almost every one of the richest, most powerful, or most famous people on earth has stayed here at one time or another. Some members of Britain's royal family consider it a home away from home. Famous American guests include the extraordinarily eccentric billionaire Howard Hughes, who stayed at the hotel off and on for almost thirty years, even though he owned several houses in Los Angeles during that time. According to the hotel's press kits, Hughes was known to order roast beef sandwiches and then require the hotel staff to hide them in trees for him. Hughes had one of his nervous breakdowns in Bungalow 4.

Bungalow 5 was favored by former *TV Guide* publisher Walter Annenberg, who used to stay at the hotel for five to six weeks every summer. Marilyn Monroe reportedly had affairs with John and Robert Kennedy in other bungalows, and Elizabeth Taylor shared bungalows there with six of her first seven husbands (Nicky Hilton, who owned his own hotels, was reportedly the lone exception).

Tom Cruise leased this home when he married Katie Holmes.

The Beverly Hills Hotel.

The hotel's celebrated Polo Lounge has been described by the *Los Angeles Times* "as much a stage and an office where entertainment industry executives make deals as it is a restaurant . . . [It is] the best improvisational theater in town."

The hotel is owned by the Sultan of Brunei, who is one of the richest men in the world. The Sultan paid $185 million for the hotel in 1987.

(DIRECTIONS: From the hotel, return to Lexington Road. Make a left on Lexington and a right onto Hartford Road, and then an immediate right on Cove Way.)

17. FORMER HOME OF SIDNEY POITIER, 1007 Cove Way

Poitier, who was the first black actor to win an Oscar (for his performance in 1963's *Lilies of the Field*), and one of Hollywood's first black directors, lived in this house for 19 years. In 1994 he sold the house to a co-chairman of Northwest Airlines.

18. HOME ONCE OWNED BY DAVID O. SELZNICK AND LATER BY ED McMAHON, 1050 Summit Drive (corner of Cove)

This mansion, originally built in the 1930s for *Gone with the Wind* producer David O. Selznick and his wife, Irene Mayer, has had a succession of celebrity owners, including Sammy Davis, Jr. (who later moved a block away); producer Freddie Fields; and Johnny Carson's sidekick Ed McMahon. McMahon sold it in 1991 as part of his divorce settlement from his wife.

CELEBRITY HOMEOWNERS ON COLDWATER CANYON include actor and one-time NRA (National Rifle Association) head Charlton Heston, who the *Los Angeles Times* reports, lives in "a highly defensible fortress atop a ridge overlooking a canyon. If push comes to shove, he can shoot marauders on their way up." His neighbors—all of whom live on the side streets off Coldwater—include Clive Barker, Candice Bergen, Tom Bosley, John Dean (yes, the Watergate conspirator who was the man most responsible for bringing down the Nixon presidency—besides Nixon himself), Barbara Eden, Carrie Fisher and her mother Debra Reynolds, Woody Harrelson, Gabe Kaplan, Christie McVie, Theresa Russell, and Esther Williams.

Former residents include Drew Barrymore, who sold a home to Ben Affleck, who turned around and sold it to late-night host Bill Maher; James Spader, who lived on Heather Road; and Rock Hudson, who, in 1985, became the first celebrity known to have died of AIDS. Hudson's estate at 9402 Beverly Crest Drive was sold to director John Landis, who in turn sold the $9 million property to Microsoft co-founder Paul Allen. Allen used the house as temporary quarters while he renovated a $20 million estate nearby.

Paul McCartney also owned a house on Heather Road that he bought from Courtney Love, who earlier purchased it from Ellen DeGeneres. An investigation by the Los Angeles District Attorney's office determined that McCartney's own-time Beatles bandmate George Harrison died in that house on November 29, 2001. Harrison's security consultants had given police a nonexistent address on Coldwater Canyon, apparently to discourage tourists from driving by the site. The consultants also misled several news outlets into reporting that McCartney had only rented the house at one time.

19. CHARLIE CHAPLIN'S "BREAKWAY" HOME,
1085 Summit Drive (corner of Cove)

Chaplin's two-story Spanish-style mansion, built in 1922, became famous because everything inside used to fall apart. "To save money on its construction," Charles Lockwood wrote in *Dream Palaces*, an intriguing book about the mansions of Beverly Hills, Chaplin "used studio carpenters when they weren't busy making sets. This seemed like a sensible plan, but it turned out to be a mistake. His carpenters had become so accustomed to putting together temporary sets that they had forgotten how to build a permanent structure. No sooner had Charlie moved into his new house than little things began to go wrong. Paneling split. Ornamental trim fell to the floors. Doors came loose on their hinges. Floors started to squeak. To Charlie's chagrin, his friends and neighbors began calling his Summit Drive dream palace Breakaway House."

After Chaplin sold the house in 1950, it passed through several hands, and at one point was owned by actor George Hamilton, who according to some, served as a front man for his friends, the Marcoses of the Philippines. Hamilton later sold the house to the daughter of former Saudi arms dealer Adnan Khashoggi. In 1991 the Republic of the Philippines successfully sued to get title of the house, and it was later sold to a private individual.

20. PICKFAIR, 1143 Summit Drive

Pickfair was the most famous house in Hollywood in the 1920s and 1930s, when it was owned by superstars Mary Pickford and Douglas Fairbanks, Sr. Charles Lockwood, in *Dream Palaces*, noted that even though "other stars' dream palaces would be architecturally more distinguished, more expensive, and even larger than

Pickfair . . . no one star's home ever claimed the same feverish public devotion year after year. Douglas Fairbanks and Mary Pickford were two of Hollywood's biggest and most enduring stars, and they were the nation's most popular couple. Pickfair was the most famous house in America, even more famous than the White House. More Americans cared about what happened there than at Warren G. Harding or Calvin Coolidge's White House."

After the couple divorced in 1936, Fairbanks moved out, and Pickford's next husband, Buddy Rogers, moved in. According to Pickford's biographer Scott Eyeman, Pickford tried "to donate the property to a charity, university or hospital after her death [in 1971], but the $300,000-$400,000 yearly upkeep dissuaded those who were approached."

In 1979 the house was sold to Los Angeles Lakers' owner Jerry Buss for $5,362,000. Buss, in turn, sold the 42-room mansion to singer Pia Zadora and her multimillionaire husband, Meshulam Riklis, for just under $7 million. Pia promptly demolished Pickfair, much to the horror of Beverly Hills preservationists, and built a new $10 million three-story Venitian-style palazoo on the site.

Less than a year after settling in, Pia divorced Riklis, moved into one of the four other houses the couple owned in the area, and left Riklis alone in the house. Riklis later sold the mansion for $18 million to a Korean businessman.

21. LAST HOME OF SAMMY DAVIS, JR., 1151 Summit Drive (across from Pickfair)

Davis died in 1990, owing the IRS $7.5 million. The IRS subsequently seized the home and sold it to a private individual as partial payment.

(DIRECTIONS: Bear left around Pickfair. Ignore the street sign, which will only confuse you—Summit turns into Pickfair—and then turn left onto San Ysidro Drive.)

22. LAST HOME OF FRED ASTAIRE, 1155 San Ysidro Drive
> Astaire's was the first home on your right.

23. LAST HOME OF DANNY KAYE, 1103 San Ysidro Drive
> Further down the street; before the intersection of San Ysidro and Tower Road.

24. FORMER HOME OF ACADEMY AWARD WINNERS SIR LAURENCE OLIVIER AND VIVIEN LEIGH, 1107 San Ysidro Drive

(DIRECTIONS: At the end of Tower Road, you will see a three-way intersection with Tower Lane on the left, Tower Grove straight ahead, and Tower Road on the right. Tower Lane is a private road on which Bruce Springsteen has a $13.9 million estate; it is not visible from the street.

Tower Grove features an extraordinary French chateau at 1400 Tower Grove, which was once the site of a house owned or leased by a succession of entertainment figures, including David O. Selznick and Elton John, and some historically interesting houses such as the site of John Barrymore's home, Bella Vista, which was also later lived in by Katherine Hepburn, Marlon Brando, and Candice Bergen.

Unfortunately, from this direction, Tower Grove is reachable only by negotiating a very steep mountainous road. The road is guaranteed to make even the most experienced driver skip a few heartbeats.

Unless you are absolutely determined to see Hollywood madam Heidi Fleiss' former home at 1270 Tower Grove Drive, you are probably better off making a left turn and continuing on to Benedict Canyon.

Once you reach Benedict Canyon, you have a choice of either going right (or north) and seeing Harold Lloyd's estate Green Acres; what you can see of the barbaric Sharon Tate/Charles Manson clan murder site; and the house that George Reeves, star of the 1950s TV show "The Adventures of Superman," lived and died in; and then U-turn on Benedict Canyon.. Or you can proceed to the $47.5 million mansion owned by David Geffen, believed to be one of the richest men in Hollywood, and then proceed to Roxbury Drive, where Lucille Ball and other celebrities lived.

The following descriptions should help you decide which option to choose.)

25. GREEN ACRES, 1740 Green Acres Drive

This 48,000 square-foot, 44-room mansion was built by silent film star Harold Lloyd, who lived here for more than 40 years until his death in 1971.

From the street all you can see are one of the twelve fountains. Not visible are the twelve formal gardens, the 120-foot-long cascading waterfall, the Olympic-size swimming pool, and the 800-foot-long canoe pond lake near the 9-hole golf course (which is adjacent to the 9-hole golf course on the former Jack Warner estate. The two courses were sometimes combined whenever the owners wanted to play a full 18 holes.)

26. SITE OF THE CHARLES MANSON CULT MURDERS, 10066 Cielo Drive

One of the most savage murders ever committed in the United States occurred here on the early morning hours of August 9, 1969. Four members of Charles Manson's cult cut telephone lines, climbed a rocky hillside, broke into the main house and slaughtered actress Sharon Tate; coffee heiress Abigail Folger; Folger's playboy lover, producer Wojtek Frykowski; internationally known hair stylist Jay Sebring; and Steven Parent, an 18-year-old college student who happened to be visiting the estate's caretaker. The murderers stabbed Tate (who was eight and a half months pregnant with director Roman Polanski's baby) 16 times, and Frykowski 51 times before writing the word "Pig" on the walls with the victims' blood.

Manson supposedly ordered his followers to kill the house's occupants because he wanted to terrify Doris Day's son, record producer Terry Melcher, whom Manson had asked to help further his recording career. Until a few months before the slaughter, Melcher had lived in the house with his then-girlfriend Candice Bergen. After Melcher moved out, Tate and Polanski, rented the house.

Even today, the murder is relived on television tabloid shows, and Manson is held up as an example of Evil personified. The house, high on the hill, was never visible from the street and was in fact torn down in 1994 when the new owners built "Villa Bella," a 17,000-square foot Mediterranean villa on the site. Tourists can only see the hillside Manson's followers had to scale in order to reach their victims.

To confuse sightseers, the new owners changed the property's address from 10050 to 10066 Cielo Drive. The humongous new mansion can be seen from Benedict Canyon or the side street, Beverly View Drive.

27. "SUPERMAN" DEATH HOUSE, 1579 Benedict Canyon Drive

George Reeves, who was television's "Superman" from 1952 to 1957, was found dead in his home in the early hours of June 16, 1959, with a .30 caliber Luger by his side.

His death was officially ruled a suicide; however, his mother never accepted the official ruling and hired private detectives in an unsuccessful attempt to prove he was murdered.

Some writers later claimed that Reeves' ghost haunts the house. The fact that a subsequent owner, screenwriter/director Phil Robinson, was inspired here to write the ghost story, *Field of Dreams* (1989), is probably just a coincidence.

[*Footnote: This house was not used for filming* Hollywoodland *(2006), which explored Reeves' life and death. The producers found a similar-looking house in Toronto.*]

28. DAVID GEFFEN'S MANSION, 1801 Angelo Drive (just west of Benedict Canyon)

Geffen, the movie/music/theater mogul who, along with Steven Spielberg and Jeffrey Katzenberg, founded DreamWorks, is one of the most powerful men in Hollywood. He spent $47.5 million for this estate, which was once owned by Warner Bros. co-founder Jack Warner. When Geffen bought it from Warner's widow he paid the highest price ever paid for a private home in the United States.

Ironically, Geffen spends most of his time at his Malibu beach house. He has half-jokingly said he is looking for an Arab shiek to take the property off his hands.

Behind the gates, the house reportedly looks like Versailles, but unfortunately from the street, only the half-block-long walls can be seen.

(DIRECTIONS: From Benedict Canyon, make a right turn onto Roxbury Drive.)

The home where the Manson cult killed actress Sharon Tate and four others. It has since been replaced by a larger mansion.

Lucille Ball's house on Roxbury Drive, as it appeared when she lived in it. The house was torn down in 1992 so a larger mansion could be built on the site. The new owners completely remodeled it, leaving only the original walls standing.

29. LAST HOME OF AGNES MOORHEAD, 1023 Roxbury Drive

Moorhead was an Academy Award-nominated actress who is perhaps best remembered as Elizabeth Montgomery's mother on the popular ABC-TV comedy "Bewitched" (1974-1982)

30. SITE OF GEORGE AND IRA GERSHWIN'S FIRST HOLLYWOOD HOME; LATER OWNED BY ROSEMARY CLOONEY, 1019 Roxbury Drive

Two doors down, at 1019 Roxbury Drive, is a house that lyricists George and Ira Gershwin leased when they moved to Los Angeles in the late 1930s. George died of a brain tumor in 1937, but Ira stayed there, until moving next door to 1021 Roxbury Drive, where the Gershwin family's Roxbury Recordings was based.

1019 Roxbury Drive was later owned by the late Jose Ferrer and his former wife, the popular singer Rosemary Clooney. Rosemary is the mother of actor Miguel and aunt of George Clooney, and when George first moved to Los Angeles in the early 1980s, he lived here with his aunt for a while. George worked as Rosemary's gofer until his acting career took off. Rosemary died in the house on June 29, 2002. The original home was torn down so a larger mansion could be built on the site.

31. HOME FORMERLY OWNED BY MADONNA, 1015 Roxbury Drive

In 2000 Madonna and her second husband, director Guy Ritchie, bought this $6.5 million eight-bedroom Spanish hacienda from Diane Keaton. Her son Rocco was born in this house. In 2003, Madonna moved to a larger residence on Sunset Boulevard, which is not visible from the street.

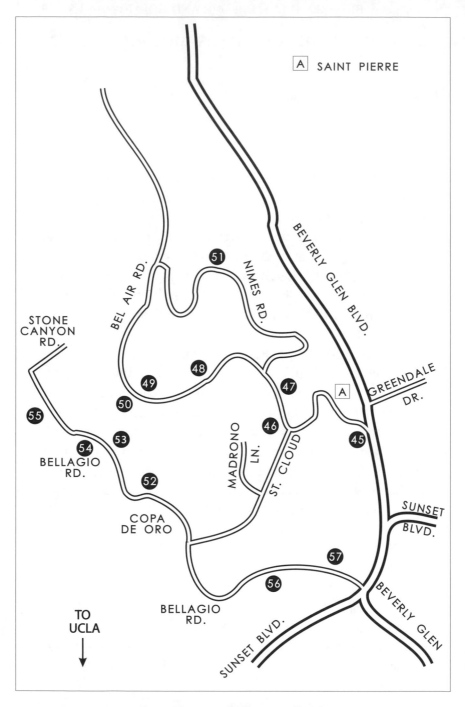

MAP 5   BEL - AIR

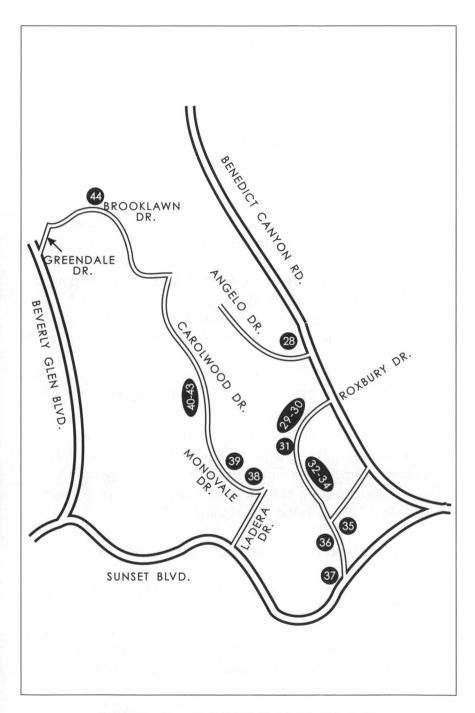

MAP 4   BEVERLY HILLS

32. HOME OF PETER FALK, 1004 Roxbury Drive
The actor is best known for his portrayal of the Los Angeles police detective, Lieutenant Columbo. His portrayal has earned him four Emmy Awards.

33. FORMER HOME OF JACK BENNY, 1002 Roxbury Drive
The comedian lived next door to Falk's current residence for almost thirty years. In 1966 he moved into an apartment, and then to his last residence, a mansion across from the Playboy Mansion (see page 54).

34. LAST HOME OF LUCILLE BALL, 1000 Roxbury Drive (corner of Lexington)
In 1955 Lucy paid $85,500 for the house. Lucy died in 1989 and three years later, the house was sold for $3.7 million.

35. SITE OF JIMMY STEWART'S LONG-TIME HOME, 918 Roxbury Drive
The two-time Academy Award-winning actor lived in a home on this site between 1949 and his death in 1997. The new owner spent $5.6 million for the property and then tore it down to build an even larger mansion. Six years later, he sold it for a reported $25 million

36. FORMER HOME OF RICKY SCHRODER, 921 Roxbury Drive
Schroder, who starred in "Silver Spoons," "NYPD Blue," and "24" lived here with his parents and his sister in the early 1990s. The 9,200-square-foot-mansion was built by the actor's parents after they tore down an existing estate that had at one time been owned by Gloria Swanson.

37. FORMER HOME OF ANGELINA JOLIE AND BILLY BOB THORNTON, 801 Roxbury Drive

The former fun couple shared vials of blood at this one-time Prohibition-era speakeasy.

(DIRECTIONS: At the end of the block is Sunset Boulevard. Make a right turn onto Sunset and continue west for about half a mile. Just past Whittier Drive, make a right onto Ladera Drive, and an immediate left onto Monovale Drive.)

38. ELVIS PRESLEY'S LAST LOS ANGELES HOME, 144 Monovale Drive

Elvis lived here from December 1967 to March 1975, when he sold the house to "Kojak" star Telly Savalas. About all that is visible from the street is Elvis' former balcony.

(Note: In what seems like a conspiracy to confuse tourists, Monovale Drive changes its name and becomes Carolwood Drive at this point.)

39. HOUSE OWNED AT VARIOUS TIMES BY GEORGE HARRISON, DAN ROWAN, AND BURT REYNOLDS, 245 Carolwood Drive

Burt Reynolds used his profits from the *Smokey and the Bandit* movies to buy this Mediterranean-style home in the mid-1980s. He lived there with his former wife, Loni Anderson, until 1990. The home was earlier owned by Dan Rowan, co-star of "Rowan and Martin's Laugh-in," and before that by George Harrison of the Beatles.

Ironically (from the outside, at least), tourists may be more impressed with the two houses next door, owned by ordinary multimillionaires, at 265 and 275 Monovale Drive. These houses sport some modern statues.

Madonna's former Spanish-style home was once owned by Diane Keaton.

Brad Pitt and Jennifer Aniston's former love nest, at 1026 Ridgedale Drive, is a few blocks off the tour map. Pitt and Aniston purchased the home for $13.5 million in 2001, and sold it five years later for just under $25 million. Frank Morgan, the actor who played the Wizard in The Wizard of Oz (1939), lived across the street at 1025 Ridgedale.

40-43. "CELEBRITY ROW": 301 TO 375 CAROL-WOOD DRIVE

Celebrities also seemed to cluster along the rest of this block. Barbra Streisand, who now lives in a three-home compound in Malibu, made 301 Carolwood Drive her primary residence between 1969 and 1997. Walt Disney lived at 355 Carolwood until his death in 1966. 375 Carolwood is the longtime home and death site of film legend Gregory Peck. In 2004 Peck's widow sold that home for $22 million.

At the end of the block—at 391 Carolwood, where the Dobermans bark the loudest and the barbed wire looks the most menacing—is Rod Stewart's former home. The popular rock star now lives in a gated community on Mulholland Drive.

(DIRECTIONS: Make a left at Brooklawn Drive and proceed 1/10 of a mile.)

44. "THE COLBYS" MANSION, 1060 Brooklawn Drive

The exterior of this house, owned by Hilton Hotels CEO Barron Hilton (and Paris' grandfather), was used as "The Colbys" residence in the "Dynasty" spin-off of that name. The house is not visible from the street.

(DIRECTIONS: Brooklawn changes its name to North Faring. As you continue, you will see on your left Harvard/Westlake School, an exclusive private preparatory school which counts among its graduates Candice Bergen, Shirley Temple, Tori Spelling, Bridget Fonda, Tracy Nelson, Sally Ride, and June Lockhart. At the stop sign, make a right turn at Greendale Drive. Then make a left onto Beverly Glen Boulevard, and an immediate right at St. Pierre Road.)

45. THE HOUSE THAT "TARZAN" NEVER LIVED IN, 414 St. Pierre Road

Tour guides invariably claim that this house was once owned by Johnny Weismuller, the most famous movie "Tarzan," and that he used to swim daily in the 150-foot-long moat-like swimming pool visible from the street. Weismuller's only biographer was unable to substantiate this claim, and Jeff Hyland, a prominent Beverly Hills realtor and author of *The Estates of Beverly Hills*, told me he believes tour guides concocted the story "because it sounded good."

Hyland reports that the house is not without significance: it was once owned by publisher William Randolph Hearst. And two famous rock-n-rollers once lived there. Mick Jagger of the Rolling Stones rented this house in 1972 when he needed an L.A. base to rehearse for a U.S. tour. John Phillips of the Mamas and The Papas had recommended the house, and Phillips later rented it himself and hosted some wild parties for his friends. In his autobiography *Papa John*, Phillips admitted he was evicted for nonpayment of rent.

(Note: St. Pierre changes its name to St. Cloud Road here.)

46. FORMER HOME OF SONNY AND CHER, 364 St. Cloud Road

In the 1991 remake of *Father of the Bride*, Steve Martin had some comic scenes here when he sneaked into his wealthy in-laws' study and tried to see their bank book.

In real life the estate was once owned by Sonny and Cher, who sold it to another former owner, *Hustler* magazine publisher Larry Flynt. In *The People vs. Larry Flynt* (1996), the mansion was featured briefly in a scene in which Woody Harrelson, playing Flynt, was taken into custody by federal marshals.

47. FORMER JOHNNY CARSON HOME, 400 St. Cloud Road

Carson bought this house in 1972 from Mervyn LeRoy, the producer of *The Wizard of Oz* (1939), and lived here until 1983. It is now occupied by Carson's ex-wife number three, Joanna.

(DIRECTIONS: Bear to the left when you reach the intersection without a sign.)

48. RONALD REAGAN'S RETIREMENT HOME, 668 St. Cloud Road

Reagan's wealthy friends bought this house for him before he left office and gave him a three-year lease with an option to buy.

The address was originally 666 St. Cloud, but Nancy Reagan, perhaps after consulting with her astrologer, had the house number changed to 668. 666 is the Sign of the Beast in the Book of Revelations in the New Testament.

(Note: St. Cloud changes its name again after the Reagans' house. It becomes Bel Air Road without warning.)

49. "BEVERLY HILLBILLIES" MANSION, 750 Bel Air Road

Adjacent to the Reagans' is the house that Jed Clampett and his family called home in "The Beverly Hillbillies," the enormously popular television show that aired from 1962 to 1970. The mansion, once known as the Kirkeby Estate, was considered to be one of the great estates of Beverly Hills until it was bought in 1986 by A. Jerrold Perenchio, a Hollywood dealmaker and chairman of

Univision, the nation's largest Spanish-language television network. The billionaire paid $13.6 million for the mansion, dismantled it, and bought the three neighboring properties for an additional $9 million, in order to build what one writer called "what by all accounts looks to be a modern monument to himself."

50. ANOTHER FORMER "MAMAS AND THE PAPAS" HOUSE, 783 Bel Air Road (corner of Strada Vecchia)

John and Michelle Phillips of the Mamas and the Papas leased this home across the street from the "Beverly Hillbillies" mansion for three years in the late 1960s before moving to the one at 414 St. Pierre Road. Previous owners include Jeanette MacDonald and Nelson Eddy.

(DIRECTIONS: Turn right on Nimes Road.)

51. HOME OF ELIZABETH TAYLOR, 700 Nimes Road

Taylor, who has overcome most of her addictions—except perhaps her addiction to publicity—lives here, just up the street from 658 Nimes Road, where composer Burt Bacharach lived for years.

Another house on the block—at 688 Nimes Road—was built for Warner Baxter, a one-time leading man whose career spanned from 1914 to 1950. You probably have not heard of him, but in 1936 Baxter was Hollywood's top money-earner. Today he serves as a reminder of just how fickle Hollywood fame can be.

His home was subsequently owned by Jack Ryan, the inventor of the Barbie doll.

An aerial view of "The Beverly Hillbillies" home and Ronald Reagan's retirement home next door.

(DIRECTIONS: Proceed south on Nimes and bear left onto St. Cloud. You will pass 400 and 364 St. Cloud again, as well as the site of a home that once stood at 332 St. Cloud, which was once owned by MGM co-founder Louis B. Mayer and later by comedian Jerry Lewis.

Just past Madrono Lane, make a right turn on Bel Air Road, and then a left on Copa De Oro Road. Do not hold up traffic, but as you turn left, glance to your right and you will see a street sign for Amapola Lane. Almost hidden from the street is a mammoth white colonial at 417 Amapola Lane, which some maps claim is the house featured on the 1990-1996 NBC comedy "The Fresh Prince of Bel-Air"). The house on the right—not visible—was the longtime former home of comedian Bob Newhart.

Continue on Copa De Oro Road.)

52. FORMER HOME OF NICOLAS CAGE, 363 Copa De Oro Road

In 1999 the Academy Award-winning actor bought this red-brick mock Tudor from entertainer Tom Jones for $6.5 million. Jones had in turn purchased the 33-room home in 1976 from another famous singer-actor, Dean Martin.

In 2006 Cage put the house on the market, asking for $35 million.

(DIRECTIONS: Make a right turn onto Bellagio Road and then another right onto Stone Canyon Road. On your left you will see Bellagio Road again. Two houses down is 10615 Bellagio Road, the last home of "Star Trek" creator Gene Roddenberry. Cary Grant also lived in that house at one point. You can make a quick left to see the house, but to continue the tour you want to keep heading north on Stone Canyon to the Hotel Bel-Air.)

53. FORMER GREER GARSON ESTATE, 680 Stone Canyon Road

Garson, a popular actress in the 1940s, won an Academy Award for her role in *Mrs. Miniver* (1942), a film that depicted England's resolve under the Blitz. She was nominated for best actress on six other occasions.

54. DON SIMPSON'S LAST HOME, 685 Stone Canyon Road

Simpson was one of the most successful and most disturbed producers in recent motion picture history. With his partner Jerry Bruckheimer, he produced hit after hit in the 1980s and early 1990s, including *Flashdance, Beverly Hills Cop, Top Gun, Days of Thunder, Crimson Tide, Dangerous Minds,* and *The Rock.*

On January 19, 1996, the 52-year-old producer's body was found in an upstairs bathroom of his mansion. Investigators were startled to discover over 2,200 (yes, 2,200) alphabetically arranged pills in a nearby closet. The coroner ruled that he died of heart failure caused by an overdose of cocaine and various prescription medications.

After his death, columnist Marilyn Beck wrote: "Simpson was lionized by hundreds of industry figures as everything from a tremendous storyteller to an unapologetic carouser. He was also a sick man heavily into sadomasochism who reportedly disfigured a prostitute during an S&M encounter."

The bestseller *You'll Never Make Love in This Town Again,* and it sequel, *Once More with Feeling,* documented other Simpson escapades with prostitutes that made this alleged disfigurement almost seem tame by comparison. The accounts are too horrific to repeat here. Even Hollywood madam Heidi Fleiss distanced herself from Simpson, insisting: "I didn't supply him with the kinky girls. Don was

Madam Alex's [her rival's] client. Actually her bread and butter."

55. HOTEL BEL-AIR, 701 Stone Canyon Road, (310) 472-1211, (800) 648-4097

Everyone raves about the Hotel Bel-Air. Charles Moore, Peter Becker, and Regula Campbell, in their guide to Los Angeles architectural highlights, *The City Observed*, call it "one of the most wonderful places in Southern California." *Conde Nast Traveler, Forbes* and *USA Today* have all rated it as the best city hotel in the United States.

Gault Millau's *The Best of Los Angeles* gushes: "If Sleeping Beauty were to wake up in Southern California, no doubt she'd find herself in the enchanted gardens of the Hotel Bel-Air. The grounds are so beautiful that they almost seem to be a fairy-tale parody. You will be charmed by the swans, the ancient trees, the eleven acres of private park, the welcoming reception with its crackling fire and the quasi-country-chateau architecture."

You will also be impressed with the celebrities you will see at the hotel. It is one of the best places in town to see celebrities, visiting European royalty, and traveling industry leaders.

(DIRECTIONS: After leaving the hotel, make a left turn and head south toward Sunset. Stone Canyon leads to Sunset; however, you do not want to go that far since you can only make a right turn at Sunset, which is a very busy street.

About 3/10 of a mile past the Hotel Bel-Air, you will reach Bellagio Road again. Make a left turn, heading east on Bellagio Road. The street signs here are very confusing, so make sure you follow the sign that reads "Sunset

Boulevard East", and bear right for a block where you will see a sign announcing the 300 block of Copa De Oro Road. Go on Copa De Oro Road for a block, then make a left at the sign which says 10400 Bellagio Road.)

56. FORMER BRIAN WILSON AND EDGAR RICE BURROUGHS HOUSE, 10452 Bellagio Road

In the 1960s Brian Wilson of the Beach Boys bought this Mediterranean villa, once owned by "Tarzan" creator Edgar Rice Burroughs, and painted it purple, upsetting the neighborhood homeowners' association to no end.

57. *"9 TO 5"* FILMING SITE, 10431 Bellagio Road

According to John Pashdag, author of *Hollywoodland USA*, this was "Dabney Coleman's house in the workplace classic *9 to 5* (1980), where Jane Fonda, Dolly Parton, and Lily Tomlin tied up their no-good boss, and hung him from the ceiling."

(DIRECTIONS: Make a right turn onto Bel Air Road, which will take you to the east gate of the community of Bel-Air. You should recognize the gates; it has been on television often enough. You may have seen it in the opening credits of "The Rockford Files."

Continue straight across Sunset Boulevard, where the street changes its name to Beverly Glen. You are now in Holmby Hills, a neighborhood that is even more expensive than Beverly Hills and Bel-Air. Take Beverly Glen Boulevard south for about half a mile; and then by the park—Holmby Park—make a left onto Club View Drive.

The first house on the left is the talk of Los Angeles.)

58. AARON SPELLING'S CHATEAU, 594 N. Mapleton Drive (corner of Club View)

Comedian David Steinberg once remarked: "In Hollywood, there's the rich. And then there's Aaron Spelling."

Spelling is a household name, and he was honored in the *Guinness Book of World Records* for being the most prolific producer of television programs of all time. Spelling is the man responsible for "The Mod Squad," "Charlie's Angels," "Fantasy Island," "The Love Boat," "Starsky and Hutch," "The Rookies," "Hart to Hart," "Hotel," "T. J. Hooker," "Vegas," "Dynasty," "Melrose Place," "Savannah," "Family," and "Beverly Hills 90210," "Seventh Heaven," and "Charmed." He once told an interviewer the reason he is so successful is because he gives people what they want: "escape from the harshness of day-to-day life."

In 1983 Spelling created what he called "our Fantasy Island" when he spent $10 million for the old Bing Crosby estate, tore it down, and built a six-acre, 123-room, $40 million mansion that is reportedly as large as a football field, or 31 times the size of the average American home. The *Los Angeles Herald Examiner* placed the 56,000-square-foot chateau in perspective by noting it was smaller than the Pentagon, but larger than the Taj Mahal, Disney's largest soundstage, or George Washington's Mt. Vernon home. The dressing room and closets of Spelling's wife, Candy, reportedly take up an entire wing. Even some of Spelling's neighbors think the size of the house is obscene.

Spelling's children, actors Tori and Randy, grew up in this house. It was here that Tori married her first husband in a $1 million ceremony. After Aaron died in the home in June 2006, Candy, supported by a staff of 28, became the home's sole occupant.

The late Aaron Spelling's home is the most extravagant private residence in Los Angeles. When daughter Tori graduated from elementary school, Aaron hired USC's marching band to celebrate the occasion.

The Playboy Mansion.

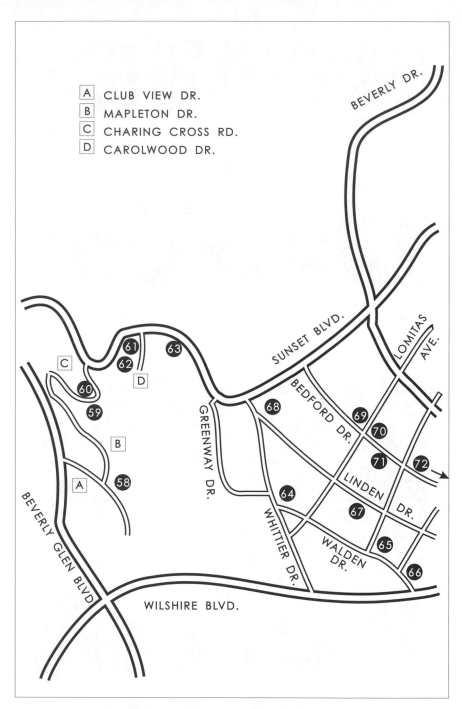

MAP 6   BEVERLY HILLS

A CLUB VIEW DR.
B MAPLETON DR.
C CHARING CROSS RD.
D CAROLWOOD DR.

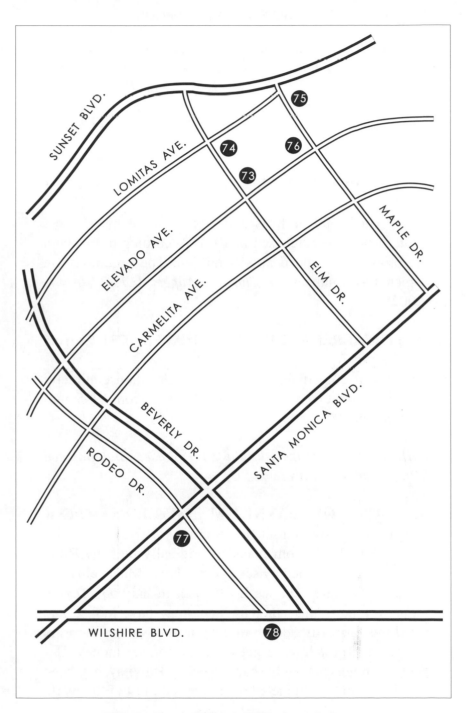

MAP 7 BEVERLY HILLS

(DIRECTIONS: After ooh-ing and aah-ing the Spelling Manor, continue north on Mapleton Drive, passing Charing Cross Road, until you see 232 S. Mapleton Drive. That is the former home of Humphrey Bogart and Lauren Bacall. Make a U-turn as soon as possible and go left onto Charing Cross Road.)

59. THE PLAYBOY MANSION, 10236 Charing Cross Road

Hugh Hefner lives and works out of his six-acre estate, which he purchased in 1971. According to tmz.com the property is valued at $50 million. The grounds were depicted as a nunnery in *Charlie's Angels 2: Full Throttle* (2002).

60. FORMER JACK BENNY ESTATE, 10231 Charing Cross Road

The comedian lived here, in this house directly across the street from the Playboy Mansion, from 1965 until his death in 1974.

(DIRECTIONS: Make a right onto Sunset, and proceed 2/10 of a mile to Carolwood Drive.

61. SITE OF JAYNE MANSFIELD'S "PINK PALACE," 10100 Sunset Boulevard

A pink 30-room mansion originally built by Rudy Vallee and later owned by sex symbol Jayne Mansfield once stood on this site. Charles Lockwood, in his book *Dream Palaces*, reports that "though Jayne may have looked and acted the part of the dumb blonde, in remodeling the Pink Palace she knew how to get the most for her money. Her Hungarian muscleman husband, Mickey Hargitay, had been a builder, and he completed or supervised most of the work.

Then Jayne's press agent, Jim Byron, asked fifteen hundred furniture and building supply houses for free samples. Think of the honor, he told them, of having your—fill in the blank—as part of the Pink Palace.

"The pitch worked. Jayne received over a hundred fifty thousand dollars' worth of free merchandise."

Mansfield's daughter, Mariska Hargitay, spent her early years here. Mariska went on to star in NBC's "Law and Order: Special Victims Unit." The house was later owned by Englebert Humperdinck, who, in 2003, sold it to new owners who tore it down to build a larger estate.

62. OWLWOOD, 141 S. Carolwood Drive

This house, directly behind the Pink Palace on the cul-de-sac south of Sunset, and not visible from the street, had a succession of celebrity owners: Sonny and Cher, Tony Curtis, and 20th Century Fox co-founder Joseph Schenck. Marilyn Monroe lived here in 1949 when she was Schenck's mistress.

63. HADERWAY HALL, 10000 Sunset Boulevard

The lifelike sculptures in front of this estate have always intrigued tourists. One of the pieces—a couple with binoculars trying to see what is in the houses—leads one to ask if anyone famous ever lived here. The answer is yes. Howard Hughes owned it at one time, and Judy Garland rented the property in 1948. Two years later, when she was separated from her second husband, director Vincente Minnelli, she recuperated from a suicide attempt here.

The statue of a cop giving a ticket to trespassers at the front gate should be self-explanatory, but one can only guess at what the statues of the two naked boys trying to peer over the fence, next to the security cameras, are supposed to represent.

(DIRECTIONS: Continue east on Sunset Boulevard for two blocks and make a right turn onto Greenway Drive, where you will see some of the prettiest lawns on the tour. You are now back in Beverly Hills. You will pass Steve Lawrence and Edie Gorme's home at 820 Greenway Drive, and a house at 813 Greenway that Debbie Reynolds once owned, and where her actress-author-script doctor daughter, Carrie Fisher, grew up. Producer Blake Edwards and his wife, Julie Andrews, also owned the house at one time.

At the stop sign make a right turn onto Whittier Drive. Just past the sign on your right that reads Walden Drive is a house on the left side of the three-way corner of Whittier Drive, Lomitas Avenue and Walden Drive. That was Buddy Hackett's house, and you will want to bear left on Walden after his house.)

64. HOME OF THE LATE BUDDY HACKETT, 800 Whittier Drive

The white elephant in front of his house was reportedly given to him as a gift by his friend Sammy Davis, Jr.

65. HOUSE AT 614 N. WALDEN DRIVE

Several blocks down the street is a house you might recognize from *Beverly Hills Cop II* (1987). Eddie Murphy pretended to be a Beverly Hills building inspector, sent the workmen remodeling it packing, and moved in himself. He told his friends on the Beverly Hills police force that it was his uncle's house.

66. THE WITCH'S HOUSE, 516 N. Walden Drive (corner of Carmelita)

This is perhaps the most unusual house on the tour of Beverly Hills. It looks like the witch's house in "Hansel and Gretel," and although the Beverly Hills Historical Society reports it has not appeared in any famous films, it did appear in some silent films in the 1920s, when the house served as an office for Irvin C. Willat Productions, a movie studio in Culver City. When the studio was sold in 1926, a former owner transplanted the house and moved it to the heart of Beverly Hills. The house was designed by set designer Henry C. Oliver, who won the first Academy Award for art direction for a long-forgotten movie named *Street Angel* (1928).

(DIRECTIONS: At the corner of Walden, make a left onto Carmelita Avenue, and another left onto Linden Drive.)

67. LAST HOME OF DAVID BEGELMAN, 705 Linden Drive

Begelman was the former head of Columbia Pictures who was convicted in 1978 of embezzling company funds. He had forged his signature on several checks, including the one which proved to be his undoing: it was a $10,000 check with actor Cliff Robertson's name on it.

The scandal, which was chronicled in David McClintock's bestseller *Indecent Exposure*, did not end Begelman's movie career. He went on to head MGM productions and Gladden Pictures and produced *Weekend at Bernie's* (1989) *and The Fabulous Baker Boys* (1989). In 1995, Begelman committed suicide just as he was about to lose his home for failing to pay the mortgage.

68. "BUGSY" SIEGEL MURDER SITE, 810 Linden Drive

Benjamin "Bugsy" Siegel—the gangster whom J. Edgar Hoover once called "the most dangerous man in

America"—was murdered in this Moorish home leased by his mistress, Virginia Hill. The 41-year-old Siegel was shot shortly before midnight on June 20, 1947, reportedly b ecause the Mafia suspected he was skimming money he had borrowed from them to build the Flamingo Hotel in Las Vegas.

Besides being the subject of a 1991 movie starring Warren Beatty and Annette Bening, Siegel's other claim to fame was that he reportedly convinced organized crime to build the first luxury hotel in Las Vegas, where gambling was legal. Some say that Las Vegas was built largely as a consequence of Bugsy's vision. In Los Angeles, he ran most of the mob's gambling and prostitution operations and socialized with movie stars like George Raft.

Time magazine called him "perhaps the most famous mobster of his era."

(DIRECTIONS: At the end of Linden Drive, make a right onto Sunset Boulevard, and then another right onto Bedford Drive.)

69. "DOWN AND OUT IN BEVERLY HILLS" HOME, 802 N. Bedford Drive
This was the house in which Richard Dreyfuss and Bette Midler lived in *Down and Out in Beverly Hills* (1985). The inside of the house and the backyard pool area were actually recreated on the Disney back lot.

70. FORMER HOME OF LANA TURNER, 730 N. Bedford Drive
Between her fourth and fifth marriages, actress Lana Turner was dating a small-time Mafia hood named Johnny Stompanato, who used the alias Johnny Valentine. Turner tried to break off the relationship, and according to the

The Witch's House in Beverly Hills.

The Beverly Hills home in which Bugsy Siegel was killed.

official version, on April 5, 1958, an angry Stompanato threatened to kill or disfigure her. Turner's daughter, Cheryl Crane, grabbed a knife and stabbed him to death in an upstairs bedroom.

Although the killing was later ruled a justifiable homicide, questions were raised as to how a 14-year-old girl could overpower the 175-pound ex-Marine. Suspicious minds wondered whether Turner killed Stompanato herself, and Crane took the blame to save her mother's career.

After Turner's death, Eric Root, her hairdresser and escort in late life (after her seventh failed marriage), claimed Lana told him: "I killed the son-of-a-bitch and I'll do it again."

71. FORMER HOME OF COMEDIAN STEVE MARTIN, 721 N. Bedford Drive

72. ONE-TIME HOME OF "THE IT GIRL," CLARA BOW, 512 N. Bedford Drive

Bow was considered the Madonna of her day (the Roaring '20s) and had quite a wild reputation. One of Hollywood's favorite legends is that she was so promiscuous that she had sex with the entire starting lineup of the USC football team. Her principal biographer, David Stenn, however, disputes the story. In *Clara Bow*, Stenn writes that Clara was just an avid football fan who used to invite the USC players and their opponents to parties at her house after the games on Saturday nights. The parties were also attended by her actress friends, including Joan Crawford. Lowry McCaslin, a sophomore end for the team, was quoted as saying: "We had a good time, but it wasn't that exciting."

(DIRECTIONS: After viewing Bow's house, make a U-turn and then right turn on to Carmelita Avenue. To see the next major concentration of show-business homes, pass Camden, Rodeo, Beverly, Canon, Crescent, Rexford, Alpine, and Foothill Drives, until you reach Elm Drive.

It should be noted in passing, though, that each of these streets has something to offer of interest. For example, a right on Camden Drive will take you to All Saints Church of Beverly Hills at 504 N. Camden Drive, where funeral services were held for Humphrey Bogart, Alfred Hitchcock and Rudolph Valentino; Rod Stewart married Rachel Hunter; Elizabeth Taylor married the first of her eight husbands; and Dudley Moore first glimpsed Bo Derek in the movie 10. A left onto Rodeo Drive will take you to the late Gene Kelly and Carl Reiner's homes at 714 and 725 Rodeo Drive, respectively. Rodeo Drive going south leads to the world-famous shopping district, usually referred to as Rodeo Drive.

A right on either Crescent or Rexford, going south, leads to the magnificent Beverly Hills City Hall. Author Jackie Collins and director Richard Benjamin live on Foothill Drive.)

73. FORMER HOME OF IVAN REITMAN, 704 N. Elm Drive

Reitman produced and directed numerous blockbuster comedies, including *Kindergarten Cop, Dave, Junior, Ghostbusters, Ghostbusters II, Twins, Legal Eagles, Evolution, Meatballs* and *Stripes.*

74. REAL LIFE "NIGHTMARE ON ELM DRIVE" HOME, 722 N. Elm Drive

One of Hollywood's most notorious murders occurred here on the night of August 20, 1989, when Jose Menendez, the 45-year-old chairman of Live

Entertainment, a division of Carolco Pictures, and his 44-year-old wife Kitty were found brutally slain in their family room. Several months later, their two sons, Lyle and Erik, were arrested after confessing to their psychiatrist that they were the killers. (The only reason the brothers were caught was because they also threatened to kill the psychiatrist if he violated doctor-patient confidentiality. The frightened shrink had his mistress (not his wife) eavesdrop on the therapy sessions in case he became their third victim. The mistress took it upon herself to report the brothers' confessions to the Beverly Hills police.)

At both their 1993 trials, in which the brothers were tried separately, and their joint 1996 retrial, the brothers admitted shotgunning their parents, but claimed they were driven to do so because Jose sexually and psychologically tortured them. The defense worked at the original trials (both juries were hung) but failed in the retrial. The brothers were convicted of first-degree murder and conspiracy to commit murder. They were sentenced to life imprisonment with no possibility of parole.

The home had an interesting history even before the Menendez family bought it. It had previously been rented to Elton John, the singer formerly known as Prince, and theatrical producer Hal Prince. The immediate previous owners were Mark Slotkin and his ex-wife, Robin Greer, who were friends with O. J. and Nicole Simpson. In 1985, before O. J. and Nicole's daughter, Sydney, was born, Robin hosted a baby shower for Nicole at the house. Although not a hooker herself, Robin subsequently gained notoriety as one of the four co-authors of the bestselling call girl tell-all *You'll Never Make Love in This Town Again*.

(DIRECTIONS: Make a right on Lomitas, and then another right on Maple Drive.)

75. LAST HOME OF GEORGE BURNS, 720 N. Maple Drive

The facade of Burns' home was used in the 1950s CBS comedy, "The Burns and Allen Show." Both Burns, who lived in the house for 60 years, and his wife, Gracie Allen, died in this home (Burns in 1996 at the age of 100; Gracie in 1964).

76. FORMER HOME OF DIANA ROSS, 701 N. Maple Drive

77. RODEO DRIVE AND NEARBY BEVERLY HILLS SHOPPING DISTRICT

As one storeowner put it: "You'll see more Rolls Royces on Rodeo Drive in ten minutes than you'll see in Cleveland, Ohio all year."

If you would like to tour this ultrachic shopping district, contact the Beverly Hills Conference & Visitors' Bureau and ask for their guide to the stores and their publication, "Beverly Hills Magazine," which includes a walking tour. The Visitors' Bureau (310-248-1015; 800-345-2210) is very helpful and offers a variety of services, including an Ambassadear program which offers multilingual docents who will host parties, take you on shopping tours, and treat you like a celebrity.

For those who wish to spend some time in the shopping district, there are a number of notable restaurants in the Beverly Hills shopping district which attract a celebrity clientele. Some of the best known are Spago Beverly Hills, 176 N. Canon Drive, (310) 385-0880; The Grill, 9560 Dayton Way, (310) 276-0615; Mr. Chow, 344 N. Camden Drive, (310) 278-9911 (where Barbra Streisand met her second husband, James Brolin, at a dinner party); and Nate 'n' Al's Delicatessen, 414 N. Beverly Drive, (310) 274-0101.

The city's concierge and goodwill ambassador, Gregg Donovan, is available to make reservations for you. He can usually be found at the corner of Rodeo Drive and Dayton Way (the entrance to 2 Rodeo Drive) greeting visitors in his red tuxedo and black silk top hat. An amateur linguist, Donovan can greet tourists in over 30 languages. He can also regal you with stories about the celebrities who shop on Rodeo Drive.

Rodeo Drive has appeared in a number of movies. In *Terminator 3* (2003) it was where a naked Kristanna Loken, the female Terminator, beamed down to Earth and hijacked a car.

78. BEVERLY WILSHIRE HOTEL, 9500 Wilshire Boulevard, (310) 275-5200, (800) 427-4354

Richard Gere and Julia Roberts stayed in the penthouse suite in *Pretty Woman* (1990). Although the outside of the hotel was used, the interior scenes were actually shot on a Disney sound stage.

Long-time residents of the hotel include Warren Beatty, who reportedly lived in Room 1001 for over a decade, and Elvis Presley, who lived in Suite 850 between 1958 and 1960.

OFF THE MAP, at 465 N. Beverly Drive (at Little Santa Monica Boulevard) is the Beverly Hills branch of the Museum of Television & Radio. The museum offers entertainment exhibits and sponsors seminars with writers, producers, directors, and actors, and other special events. For information call (310) 786-1000.

The Four Seasons Hotel at Beverly Hills, 300 S. Doheny Drive, is another great place for celebrity-watching. Many studios hold their press junkets there, so there is always a chance you will see a familiar face at the hotel's bar or restaurant.

Beverly Hills Ambassador Gregg Donovan at 2 Rodeo Drive.

Beverly Wilshire Hotel

QUITE A FEW OTHER CELEBRITIES OWN (OR HAVE OWNED) HOMES IN BEVERLY HILLS, including Neil Diamond and the late Abigal van Buren ("Dear Abby"), who lived on the side streets near the Beverly Hills Hotel; Lara Flynn Boyle; Dixie Carter and Hal Holbrook; Jackie Chan; Simon Cowell; Dr. Phil McGraw; Mary Hart; Lenny Kravitz; Steve Martin; George Michael (who was arrested for indecent behavior in the park across the street from the Beverly Hills Hotel); Priscilla Presley; Don Rickles; Pete Sampras; Ringo Starr; Sharon Stone; Mark Wahlberg; Sela Ward; and Raquel Welch.

In 1954 Joe DiMaggio and Marilyn Monroe lived for five months at 508 N. Palm, one street east of Maple Drive. It is often referred to as their "Honeymoon Home" and five decades later, it still attracts tourists.

Monica Lewinsky, the White House intern whose affair with President Bill Clinton led to Clinton's impeachment, spent her formative years at 604 N. Hillcrest Drive. Monica was in high school in 1988 when her parents divorced and sold the house.

Richard Nixon, a president who was involved in far more serious crimes, is another former resident of Beverly Hills. He lived at 410 Martin Lane in 1962, the year he ran for governor of California.

BRENTWOOD

1. NICOLE BROWN SIMPSON/RON GOLDMAN MURDER SITE, 879 S. Bundy Drive

The three-story townhouse owned by O. J. Simpson's ex-wife Nicole became a macabre tourist attraction after she was murdered there on June 12, 1994, along with Ron Goldman, an acquaintance who worked at Brentwood's Mezzaluna restaurant. Nicole had dined at the restaurant with her family earlier that evening, and Goldman drove to the condo after he got off work to return to Nicole her mother's eyeglasses, which had been left behind after the dinner.

The condominium is within a short distance of Nicole's previous residence, a house at 325 S. Gretna Greene Way. That was the site of Nicole's infamous 1993 911 call to the police. In that call, Nicole pleaded with police to come to the house before O. J. harmed her, as he had in the past. O. J. reportedly broke down the back door of that residence.

After the murders, a Century City attorney bought the condo, installed landscaping, reconfigured the walkway, and changed the address from 875 to 879 S. Bundy to make it difficult for tourists to recognize the murder scene.

Mezzaluna, the so-called "murder restaurant" (11750 San Vicente Boulevard), closed in 1997. According to its former owner, hordes of tourists kept the local clientele away, and when the tourists stopped coming, the locals never came back.

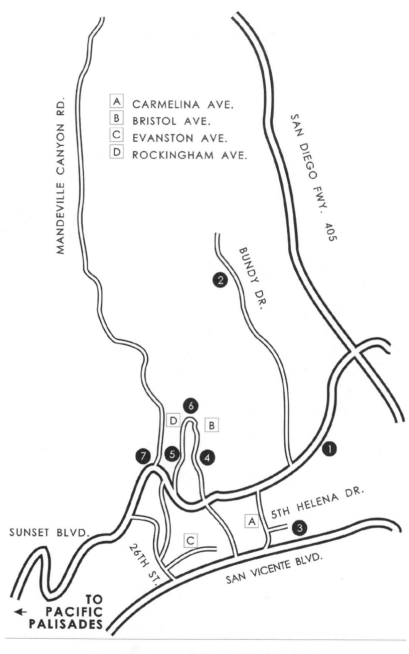

A CARMELINA AVE.
B BRISTOL AVE.
C EVANSTON AVE.
D ROCKINGHAM AVE.

MANDEVILLE CANYON RD.

SAN DIEGO FWY. 405

BUNDY DR.

SUNSET BLVD.

26TH ST.

5TH HELENA DR.

SAN VICENTE BLVD.

TO
← PACIFIC
PALISADES

MAP 8   BRENTWOOD

2. *"SIX CRISES"* HOME, 901 N. Bundy Drive

Richard Nixon leased this house after losing the 1960 presidential election. He wrote *Six Crises* here.

3. MARILYN MONROE HOME, 12305 Fifth Helena Drive (off Carmelina Street)

Although some conspiracy theorists allege that Monroe was murdered here because of her affairs with first John and then Robert Kennedy, Monroe died (at least according to the official autopsy report) of a drug overdose in her bedroom on August 4, 1962. She lived in this house alone with her dog Maf (short for Mafia), which she received as a present from Frank Sinatra.

4. "MOMMIE DEAREST" HOUSE, 426 N. Bristol Avenue

In her book *Mommie Dearest,* Joan Crawford's daughter Christina told of being abused in this house while growing up.

5. SHIRLEY TEMPLE'S CHILDHOOD HOME, 209 N. Rockingham Avenue

Until 1951, Shirley lived at 209 N. Rockingham, while her parents lived next door at 227 N. Rockingham.

6. SITE OF O. J. SIMPSON'S MANSION, 360 (now 380) N. Rockingham Avenue

On June 17, 1994, a suicidal O. J. Simpson surrendered to police in the driveway of his estate after evading arrest earlier that day for the murder of his ex-wife, Nicole Brown Simpson, and her friend, Ronald Goldman. The surrender, which was witnessed by a nationally televised audience of 95 million, climaxed an extraordinary day in which Simpson became a fugitive from justice and

Marilyn Monroe died in this Brentwood home.

In the 1990s, when she starred on the most popular sitcom on TV, Roseanne lived at 12916 Evanston Drive. She now lives in Rolling Hills, California.

was chased by police over 60 miles of Southland freeways before returning home.

Police had arrested Simpson because investigators had found on his property a bloodstained glove, which matched another glove left at the murder scene, and blood stains in Simpson's driveway and bathroom.

At the crime scene, police also found Simpson's blood, a knit cap by Goldman's feet that contained hairs that matched Simpson's, and fibers like those from his car. Additional evidence was found on Ron Goldman's shirt (Simpson's hairs and fibers that matched his clothing) and in Simpson's Ford Bronco (a mixture of blood which matched both the victims and Simpson's).

Despite this overwhelming circumstantial evidence of guilt, attorneys for the Hall of Fame football player turned sportscaster and actor managed to convince a jury that the evidence was so compromised that Simpson should be acquitted.

Sixteen months later, in February 1997, a civil jury determined that Simpson caused Ron and Nicole's deaths and awarded the victims' families $33.5 million.

As a result of the judgment, Simpson was forced to move from his mansion, which was subsequently torn down by the new owners. Nevertheless, Simpson still managed to rent a $6,200-a-month mountaintop house in Pacific Palisades in Tom Hanks, Tom Cruise, and Steven Spielberg's neighborhood. He subsequently moved to Florida, where his house and income were protected against civil judgments. The Goldmans never collected a cent.

7. MANDEVILLE CANYON ROAD

This pretty canyon road, just north of Sunset, has always attracted an unusual number of celebrities. Former residents include Tom Selleck; Mark Harmon and Pam

Dawber; Steven Seagal; and directors Barry Levinson and John Badham. The late John Candy, lived at 1630 Mandeville Canyon; Michael Douglas, 2915 Mandeville Canyon; and Gregory Peck lived at 2359.

"Bonanza" star Lorne Greene lived at 2090 Mandeville Canyon Road for years. Dick Powell once lived on the 3100 block of Mandeville Canyon Road—and a location scout told me that the exterior of his house was used as Robert Wagner and Stephanie Powers' house in the 1979-1984 ABC adventure series "Hart to Hart." It is not, however, visible from the street.

Just off Mandeville Canyon, at the northeast corner of Chalon, is an exclusive gated community, Brentwood Country Estates, where Arnold Schwarzenegger, and his wife, Maria Shriver, currently live. The Schwarzeneggers live in a 11,000 square foot house valued in the early 2000s at $11 million.

OTHER CELEBRITIES WHO OWN HOMES IN BRENTWOOD include Anne Archer, Bea Arthur, Kate Beckinsale, James Belushi, Peter Bogdanovich, George Carlin, Stephen Collins, Robert Culp, Tim Daly, Ted Danson, Kim Delaney, Phyllis Diller, Calista Flockhart, Harrison Ford, Glenn Frey, James Garner, Jennifer Garner and Ben Affleck, Dustin Hoffman, Janet Jackson, Angela Lansbury, Anthony LaPlagia, Dylan McDermott, Kate Mulgrew, Randy Newman, Ken Olin and Patricia Wettig, Michael Ovitz, Rob Reiner, Mimi Rogers, Rene Russo, Garry Shandling, Courtney Thorne-Smith, John Travolta, Robert Wagner and Jill St. John, and Betty White.

O. J. Simpson's mug shot

Arnold Schwarzenegger's home in Brentwood

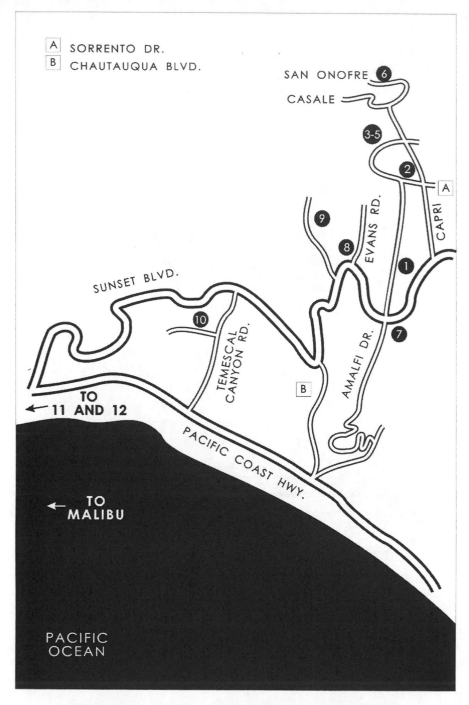

MAP 9 PACIFIC PALISADES

PACIFIC PALISADES

1. THE FIRST HOME OWNED BY RONALD AND NANCY REAGAN IN PACIFIC PALISADES, 1258 Amalfi Drive
The Reagans lived here from 1953 to 1956.

2. FORMER TOM CRUISE-NICOLE KIDMAN HOME, 1525 Sorrento Drive
The couple lived here throughout the 1990s and sold it after their divorce in 2001.

3. FORMER HOME OF SYLVESTER STALLONE, 1570 Amalfi Drive
When Stallone lived here, he constantly fought with his neighbors (including sports broadcaster Vin Scully) over the size of his trees and gates.

4. HOME OWNED BY STEVEN SPIELBERG, 1515 Amalfi Drive
Five-and-a-half foot tall gates block the view of this extraordinary mansion, which was featured in the May 1989 and November 1994 issues of *Architectural Digest*. Spielberg told the magazine: "The history of the house attracted me instinctively. It was important for me to know that David Selznick had lived there during the time he produced *Gone With The Wind*." Other previous owners include Douglas Fairbanks, Jr.; and Cary Grant and Barbara Hutton. Spielberg purchased the mansion in 1985 from singer Bobby Vinton.

5. HOME ONCE OWNED BY DAVID NIVEN AND LATER BY WHOOPI GOLDBERG, 1461 Amalfi Drive

Niven lived here, in what he dubbed "The Pink House," from 1945 to 1960. In 1994, subsequent owner Whoopi Goldberg married Lyle Trachtenberg here. The marriage lasted a year and Whoopi moved to Malibu.

6. FORMER RONALD REAGAN HOUSE, 1669 San Onofre Drive

Ronald and Nancy Reagan bought this ranch house in November 1955 and lived here when he was elected president in 1980.

7. "DOOGIE HOWSER, M.D." HOUSE, 796 Amalfi Drive

Producer Steven Bochco used this house in his former neighborhood for exterior shots of the Howser residence.

8. EVANS ROAD, Pacific Palisades

Driving on this private road is prohibited by law, and if you get caught trespassing—and are convicted—you could be fined as much as $500 and thrown in jail for a year. Only residents and their guests can drive by the four contiguous mansions, valued at $18 million, formerly owned by Arnold Schwarzenegger and Maria Shriver.

Schwarzenegger originally bought the mansion pictured on page 76 for an estimated $3 million, and then spent another $5 million to buy the homes of his one-time next-door neighbors, actors John Forsythe and Daniel J. Travanti. The fourth house in his compound was previously owned by a part-owner of the Pittsburgh Pirates. In 2002 the couple moved to a gated community.

This was Arnold Schwarzenegger and Maria Shriver's main residence until 2002. They now live in a gated community in Brentwood.

Thelma Todd's Sidewalk Café, circa 1935.

9. WILL ROGERS STATE HISTORIC PARK, 14253
Sunset Boulevard, (310) 454-8212

Situated in this popular public park is the ranch house of humorist and silent screen star Will Rogers, who lived there from 1924 until his death in a plane crash in 1935. After his widow's death in 1944, the grounds were donated to the State of California for use as a public park. The house contains artifacts and memorabilia pertaining to Rogers' career.

In 1984 the park doubled as Golden State Park in San Francisco, where the Klingon ship, commandeered by the "Star Trek" crew, set down in *Star Trek IV: The Voyage Home*. For house hours and information call (310) 454-8212. There is a parking fee.

10. PACIFIC PALISADES HIGH SCHOOL, 15777
Bowdoin Street (west of Temescal Canyon Road and visible from Sunset Boulevard)

This is the high school immortalized by Michael Medved and David Wallechinsky in their bestseller *What Really Happened to the Class of '65?* Their book was a follow-up to a *Time* magazine cover story about American teenagers in the sixties which focused on Pali High's senior class of 1965.

Pali alumni include Christie Brinkley, Jeff Bridges, Anthony Edwards, Katey Sagal, Forest Whitaker, Penelope Ann Miller, and the Bangles' Susanna Hoffs. Jennifer Jason Leigh was a Pali dropout.

The school has also appeared in several movies, including Lindsay Lohan's Sunset Ridge High School in *Freaky Friday* (2003).

(DIRECTIONS: To continue the Pacific Palisades tour and head toward Malibu, make a right turn at the intersection of Sunset and Pacific Coast Highway.)

11. SITE OF THELMA TODD'S ROADSIDE CAFE,
17575 Pacific Coast Highway (and 17531 Posetano Road, Todd's apartment above the cafe)

In the 1930s this building housed a popular celebrity hangout, Thelma Todd's Roadside Cafe, owned by Todd, a popular actress who appeared in 108 films. On December 16, 1935, the 29-year-old Todd was found dead in the garage of her apartment above the cafe. She was found slumped behind the wheel of her Lincoln; there was blood on her mink coat and evening dress, the car, the garage floor, and on her head and face. Amazingly, the Los Angeles County coroner ruled her death an accidental suicide, leading to allegations that she may have been murdered, with the murder covered up by the police. Todd's ex-husband was connected with the mob, and rumors persisted that the mob wanted to use the cafe as a gambling den; that Todd refused, and was killed for not going along with the plan.

12. MEL GIBSON GOES NUTS, intersection of Pacific Coast Highway and Tuna Canyon

This intersection, located just two miles north of where Pacific Coast Highway meets Sunset Boulevard, is where, in the early hours of July 28, 2006, Mel Gibson was pulled over by California Highway Patrol officers for speeding and suspicion of drunk driving. The actor-director, whose blood alcohol level was twice as high as the legal limit, tried to walk away from officers, called a female officer "sugar tits," and blamed the world's problems on the Jewish people, apparently after he sensed that the officer who stopped him was Jewish.

Gibson had long been one of the strongest supporters of the L.A. County Sheriff's Office, which initially tried to cover up his bad behavior. Gibson later apologized, but many Jews, already wary of Gibson because of his movie *The Passion of the Christ* (2004) and the fact his father was a Holocaust-denier, felt he was only revealing his true colors.

The Jewish deputy who made the arrest was later investigated and harassed by his superiors, who suspected he was the one who leaked the full arrest report instead of the sanitized version released by his superiors.

OTHER CELEBRITIES WHO OWN HOMES IN PACIFIC PALISADES include Kim Carnes, Billy Crystal, Cuba Gooding, Jr., Peter Graves, Kate Hutton, Michael Keaton, Sugar Ray Leonard, Julia Louis-Dreyfuss, Marsha Mason, Stevie Nicks, Sydney Pollack, Michael Richards, Bob Saget, Brooke Shields, Patrick Stewart, Tracy Ullman, and Forest Whitaker.

MALIBU

1. CARBON BEACH

Carbon Beach is sometimes referred to as "Billionaires Beach" or "Deal Beach" since so many entertainment industry executives do business from their summer or weekend beach homes here. "Dealers" include two of DreamWorks co-founders, Jeffrey Katzenberg and David Geffen; producer Jerry Bruckheimer, several entertainment attorneys and heads of talent agencies; software magnate Larry Ellison, who owns at least five houses, and a number of other nonindustry billionaires.

Carbon Beach also has its fair share of stars. Johnny Carson spent most of the 1980s at 22240 Pacific Coast Highway, which is where he spotted his fourth and final wife, Alex Maas, walking along the beach in front of his house. Carson later sold the house to John McEnroe for a reported $1.85 million and six tennis lessons. "Johnny was so serious about the lessons," Carson biographer Laurence Leamer wrote in *King of the Night* "that the stipulation was included in the sales contract."

In 1991 Janet Jackson bought *Terminator* and *Aliens* producer Gail Ann Hurd's house down the street for what was then a bargain $4.5 million. (Prices now start at around $20 million.)

Bruce Willis and Demi Moore owned a home at 22470 Pacific Coast Highway between 1987 and 1999.

The late comedian Flip Wilson insisted that his house at 21970 Pacific Coast Highway was once haunted by

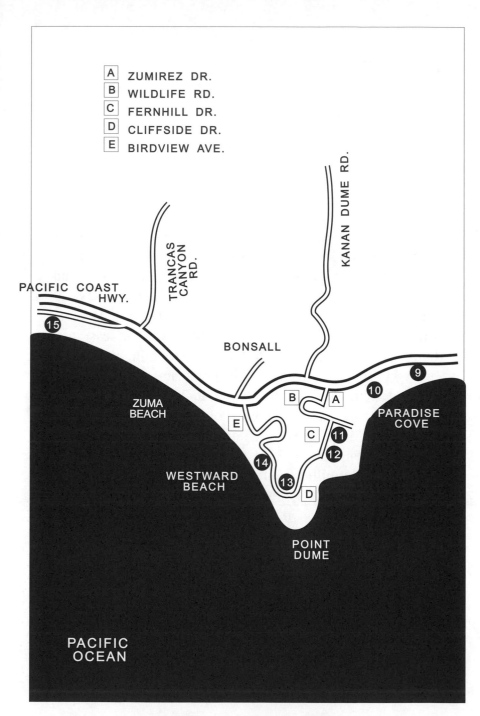

A ZUMIREZ DR.
B WILDLIFE RD.
C FERNHILL DR.
D CLIFFSIDE DR.
E BIRDVIEW AVE.

KANAN DUME RD.

TRANCAS CANYON RD.

PACIFIC COAST HWY.

BONSALL

ZUMA BEACH

PARADISE COVE

WESTWARD BEACH

POINT DUME

PACIFIC OCEAN

MAP 11   MALIBU

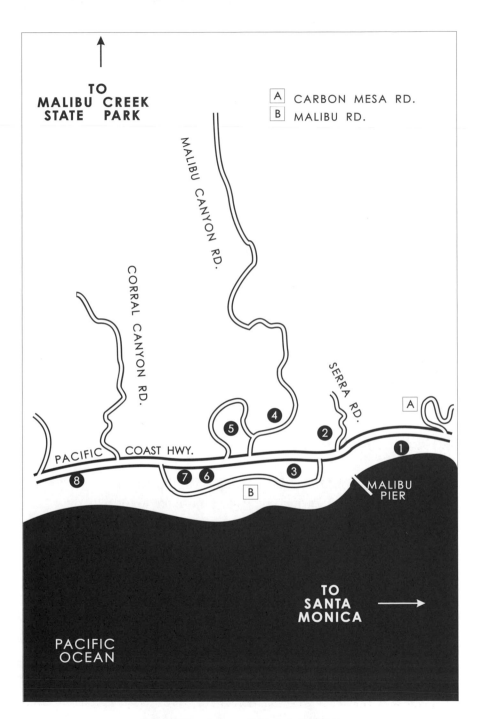

TO
**MALIBU CREEK
STATE PARK**

A CARBON MESA RD.
B MALIBU RD.

MALIBU CANYON RD.

CORRAL CANYON RD.

SERRA RD.

A

PACIFIC COAST HWY.

⑤ ④ ②

⑧ ⑦ ⑥ ③ ①

B

MALIBU
PIER

TO
**SANTA
MONICA** →

**PACIFIC
OCEAN**

MAP 10   MALIBU

a previous owner, actor Laurence Harvey. Wilson promised to haunt the house himself after his own death.

You can walk in front of the beach homes by taking the unofficially named "Zonker Harris Access Way," an entryway between 22126 Pacific Coast Highway and the Windsail Apartments. The access way is an homage to a surfer-slacker character in the cartoon strip "Doonesbury."

2. SERRA RETREAT, on Serra Road just past the Malibu Pier

About seven miles north of Carbon Beach is Serra Retreat, a beautiful private community built around a Franciscan spiritual retreat—also called Serra Retreat—nestled in Malibu Canyon. (This was portrayed as the convent featured in the 1967-70 ABC-TV comedy "The Flying Nun" starring Sally Field.)

Mel Gibson's home is in this community. This is also where Britney Spears and Kevin Federline lived, as well as Dick van Dyke and director James Cameron.

A security guard at the front gate discourages looky-loos from sightseeing.

3. MALIBU COLONY (at 23554 Malibu Road)

Gates and armed security guards keep tourists out of this exclusive and snooty (according to some realtors) celebrity enclave. Colonists include Tom Hanks, John McEnroe (who moved here after selling Carson's Carbon Beach home), Rob Reiner, and Sting.

4. HODGES CASTLE, 23800 Malibu Crest Drive

A real castle, formerly owned by a dentist, Dr. Hodges, and later by the daughter of an exiled Iranian oil minister. (You will see a few more castles when you take the Hollywoodland tour.)

Halle Berry, who, as a 21-year-old struggling model, lived in a New York City homeless shelter, now owns an $8 million glass, stainless steel, and granite second home in a security-guarded street in Malibu, where she lived next door to Bruce Willis.

During her marriage to Kevin Federline, Spears lived next door to director James Cameron in the gated community Serra Retreat.

Patterned after a 13th-Century Scottish castle, the Hodges Castle is perched on a hillside north of Pacific Coast Highway, and can be seen from several directions, including from the gates of Malibu Colony and from behind the Malibu County Mart.

5. PEPPERDINE UNIVERSITY, 24255 Pacific Coast Highway

Prestigious, picturesque and private, Pepperdine is a popular filming site. "Battle of the Network Stars" was filmed here. Famous alumni include Brandy and twin actresses Tia and Tamera Mowry of "Sister, Sister."

6. FORMER HOME OF RICH LITTLE, 24734 Pacific Coast Highway

Litttle now resides in Las Vegas.

7. HOME AT 24834 PACIFIC COAST HIGHWAY

In Postcards From the Edge (1990), Meryl Streep shot at Dennis Quaid in this house, where Quaid's character was supposed to have lived.

8. GULLS WAY, 26800 Pacific Coast Highway

Brian Keith, playing Judge Milton C. Hardcastle, lived in this house in the 1983 to 1986 TV series "Hardcastle and McCormick."

9. MALIBU GOLD COAST, 27700 to 27944 Pacific

You will not find the "Malibu Gold Coast" or any points north of Pepperdine on the Auto Club city maps. But if you continue north on Pacific Coast Highway, you will pass a stretch of land that talent agent Charles Stern dubbed "The Malibu Gold Coast"—which describes the beachfront strip of land that runs for a mile or so between his property on private Escondido Beach Road and Paradise Cove to the north.

Celebrity residents include America's oldest teenager, Dick Clark (27700 Pacific Coast Highway), and producer Jerry Weintraub, who threw parties for his friend, then-President George Bush, at his home, "Blue Heaven," at 27740 Pacific Coast Highway. Producer Blake Edwards and his wife, actress Julie Andrews, lived for years at a home at 27944 Pacific Coast Highway. Their home has since been torn down and replaced with an even larger mansion.

10. PARADISE COVE

If you turn left at Paradise Cove Road, and head toward the restaurant at 28128 Pacific Coast Highway, you will see where a number of popular TV shows and movies have been filmed. James Garner parked his trailer in the parking lot adjacent to the restaurant in NBC-TV's "The Rockford Files" (1974-80), and William Conrad's house in CBS' "Jake and the Fatman" (1987-92) was the first house on the left of the restaurant.

The 1950s Frankie Avalon/Annette Funicello films *Beach Party, Muscle Beach Party, Beach Blanket Bingo*, and *Back to the Beach,* and *Lethal Weapon 4* (1998) were all filmed here. In *Indecent Proposal* (1993), Woody Harrelson proposed to Demi Moore on the pier.

According to Art Fein's *L.A. Musical History Tour,* "the Beach Boys posed for their first album cover on this stretch of beach."

(Note: The following three houses are located in an area known as Point Dume, south of Pacific Coast Highway.)

A view of the homes in Malibu Colony.

The former Unger Estate (left) and Johnny Carson's home (right).

11. LAST HOME OF JOHNNY CARSON, 6962 Wildlife Road

Carson purchased this spectacular retreat house, which is situated 200 feet over a cliff, for just under $8.9 million in 1985. According to his biographer Laurence Leamer, Carson also "bought the land across the street, and at a cost of several million dollars constructed one of the most remarkable private tennis courts in the world. It was not so much a court as a mini-stadium, built recessed so that passers-by could not catch even a glimpse of Johnny playing each day."

Carson died in 2005 at the age of 79. Two years later, the house was purchased by movie executive and Carson fan for $38 million.

12. THE FORMER UNGER ESTATE, 6970 Wildlife Road

In 1985 Madonna and Sean Penn were married at this palatial clifftop home owned by a friend of the Penn family, Dan Unger, who has been variously identified as a real estate developer and an attorney. In *Madonna Unauthorized*, Christopher Andersen described "the scene at the Unger home more closely resembled a war than a wedding. While armed security guards scanned the horizon with infrared binoculars looking for intruders—namely, members of the press—their blazer-clad brethren checked the credentials of each guest who passed through the ten-foot-high steel gates. Reporters dressed as waiters climbed over the walls, picked up silver trays, and began serving sushi and Cristal champagne to the guests . . . The publicity-loathing Penn, enraged at the presence of the helicopters, ran down to the beach and scrawled FUCK OFF in twenty-five foot letters in the sand. For nearly a half hour, he paced up and down the beach, shaking his fists at the choppers and yelling profanities. 'He went, in the words of one guest, 'completely nuts' . . . and emptied his gun at the helicopter."

13. FORMER HOME OF CHER, 29149 Cliffside Drive
The Academy Award-winning actress and entertainer, who was born Cheryl Sarkisian in 1946, owned this house between 1990 and 1999.

14. WESTWARD BEACH
Music videos filmed here include Madonna's "Cherish" and Vanessa Williams' "Dreamin." At the end of the parking lot is the spot where Charlton Heston found the remnants of the Statue of Liberty in the 1968 classic *Planet of the Apes*.

15. BROAD BEACH (six miles north of Paradise Cove)
It would probably be fair to say that more celebrities own homes on this mile-and-a-half stretch of land than in any other concentrated living area in the world. Pierce Brosnan, Craig Ferguson, Whoopi Goldberg, Kelsey Grammer, Goldie Hawn, Kate Hudson, Sylvester Stallone, Jon Bon Jovi, Grant Tinker, Michael Ovitz, Danny DeVito, Dick Martin, Steve Lawrence and Edie, Dustin Hoffman, Ralph Edwards, Robert Redford, Ray Romano, Neil Simon, Eddie van Halen and Valerie Bertenelli, as well as the late Carroll O'Connor, Jack Lemmon, Walter Matthau, and Frank Sinatra all own or have owned weekend or summer houses here.
A few celebrities, including director/producer James L. Brooks and Steven Spielberg, own more than one house on the beach. Mel Gibson, Charlie Sheen, and basketball coach Pat Riley, are among the celebrities who own beachfront houses on the side streets off Broad Beach.
In July 1996, Broad Beach became the site of the infamous "Goldilocks Incident," in which a couple discovered that a strange man had wandered into their house, neatly folded his pants over a chair, and gone to sleep in their son's bed. That man was Academy Award-nominated actor, and

apparently heroin-addicted, Robert Downey, Jr., who had mistaken their home for a house he was leasing 17 houses away. The incident prompted Jay Leno to joke: "Do you know what the hottest new business on Hollywood Boulevard is? Selling Robert Downey, Jr., a map to his own home."

(Note: Tourists who wish to see celebrity houses up close can do so by walking through a public walkway next to 31346 Broad Beach. The fence is unlocked between sunrise and sunset. Although security guards hired by the homeowners have been known to harass beachgoers, there are signs indicating where nonresidents can walk along the shoreline without trespassing.)

Reminder: Do not approach or otherwise disturb the occupants of any of the houses in this book. Stay away from the stars for your own safety!

The climatic scene in the classic *Planet of the Apes* (1968). Charlton Heston realized he had returned to Earth—and mankind had destroyed itself in his absence.

More celebrities own homes on Malibu's Broad Beach than anywhere else in the world.

SANTA MONICA AND VENICE

1. OCEAN FRONT WALK (sometimes referred to as the Venice Boardwalk, Ocean Front Walk extends from Washington Boulevard in Marina del Rey to Marine Street in Santa Monica)

Most of the walk is along Venice Beach, which is famous for its street entertainers, bodybuilders, roller skaters, and the ubiquitous drug pushers, who can often be identified by pagers on their belts. On weekends the atmosphere is carnival-like.

The beach here has appeared in countless movies (including 1992's *White Men Can't Jump*) and television shows. Fans of "Three's Company," starring John Ritter, Suzanne Somers and Joyce DeWitt, may recall the beach bicycle scenes in the opening credits.

2. BALLERINA CLOWN, corner of Rose Avenue and Main Streets

"At the corner of Rose & Main," *Travel and Leisure* magazine notes, "is one of LA's newest landmarks, artist Jonathan Borofsky's monumental sculpture known variously as the Clown, the Dancer or 'that horrid thing.' It's a surreal combination of a clown's head, with a sad Emmett Kelly face, and the body of a tutu-clad ballerina: It's shocking, it's original, it offends the hell out of people. Whatever your opinion, the Ballerina Clown (its real name) serves as a great meeting place, since everyone knows where it is."

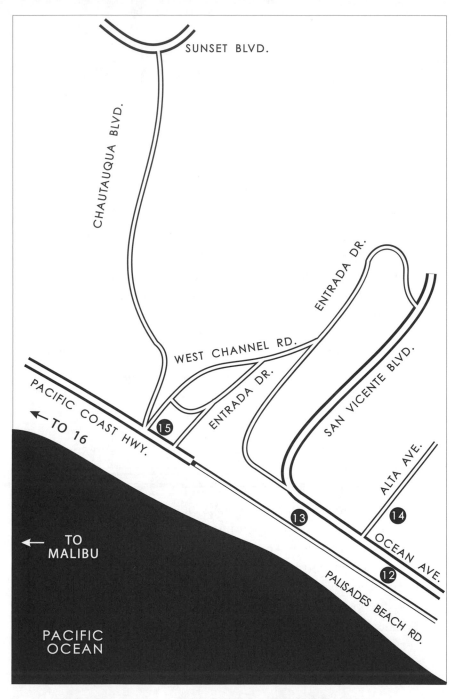

SUNSET BLVD.

CHAUTAUQUA BLVD.

ENTRADA DR.

WEST CHANNEL RD.

ENTRADA DR.

SAN VICENTE BLVD.

PACIFIC COAST HWY.

← TO 16

ALTA AVE.

OCEAN AVE.

PALISADES BEACH RD.

← TO MALIBU

PACIFIC OCEAN

15

13

14

12

MAP 13   SANTA MONICA

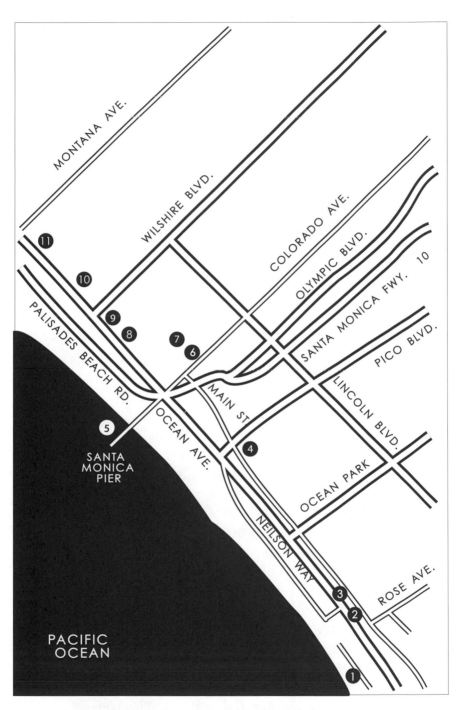

MAP 12   SANTA MONICA

(Neighborhood note: Just down the street, on the block past the clown—is where the heard, but not seen, explosion of Keanu Reeves' bus occurred early in *Speed* (1994).

Cattycorner to the Clown, in the middle of the 3000 block of Main, is the architecturally famous "Binocular Building" designed by L.A.'s own Frank Gehry. This building, built in the shape of 45-foot-tall binoclaurs, houses the L.A. offices of Chiat/Day's advertising firm.)

3. SCHATZI ON MAIN, 3110 Main Street, (310) 399-4800

When he was still an actor, Arnold Schwarzenegger frequently dined at this restaurant, which he formerly co-owned with his wife, Maria Shriver. Schwarzenegger still owns the entire block-long red-brick shopping complex (Main Street Plaza), which consists of three separate buildings. One of the buildings housed his production offices.

4. SANTA MONICA CIVIC AUDITORIUM, 1855 Main Street (at Pico)

Site of the Academy Awards presentations from 1961 to 1968.

The 1996-97 civil trial which found O. J. Simpson responsible for the deaths of his ex-wife Nicole, and Ron Goldman, was held at the county courthouse next door. The courthouse was also the site of Harrison Ford's 1983 marriage to *E.T.* screenwriter Melissa Mathison.

5. SANTA MONICA PIER, end of Colorado Avenue (at Ocean Avenue)

Featured in countless television shows and movies, including *Ruthless People; The Sting; The Net; They Shoot Horses, Don't They?; Mighty Joe Young; The Majestic;* and

The Ballerina Clown in Venice.

The Santa Monica Pier.

Funny Girl. According to Steven Gaines, author of *Heroes and Villains: The True Story of the Beach Boys,* Brian Wilson once jumped off the pier in a suicide attempt, but was rescued by his brother Dennis.

6. SANTA MONICA PLACE (bounded by 4th and Colorado; 2nd and Broadway)

The mall scenes in *Terminator II* (1991) were filmed here, including the fight scenes between the two Terminators, which were filmed in the back hallways, and a scene in which Schwarzenegger was thrown through the window of a clothing store, the Oak Tree. The video arcade was built specially for the movie in an empty storefront. (The producers used the Northridge Mall at 9301 Tampa Avenue, Northridge, for the exterior shots).

Also filmed here was the 1990 feature *Internal Affairs.* A police station was built on the roof of the parking lot. Richard Gere beat up Andy Garcia in an elevator built on the same spot.

7. THIRD STREET PROMENADE (between Broadway and Wilshire Boulevard)

In *A Very Brady Sequel* (2003), the Brady Bunch broke into song outside the former Woolworth's at this popular outdoor mall. The promenade features a variety of theaters, bookstores, gift shops, clothing stores and restaurants.

One of the restaurants, the Broadway Café, was also the site of Robert DeNiro's first meeting with Amy Brenneman in *Heat* (1987).

8. SHANGRIA-LA HOTEL, 1301 Ocean Ave.

This seven-story Art Deco hotel has been a celebrity hangout for years. Bill Murphy, Diane Keaton, and others have all stayed long-term.

9. LAWRENCE WELK PLAZA, 100 Wilshire Boulevard (at Ocean Avenue)

The 22-story General Telephone Building, now part of the Lawrence Welk Plaza, served as the hospital front for the television series "Marcus Welby, M.D."

10. 1221 OCEAN AVE., 1221 Ocean Ave.

This condominium, named after its street address, has been home to several celebrities, including Alanis Morrisette and Tom Arnold. In the early 2000s Britney Spears lived here while her house in Malibu was being remodeled. Photos of Spears outside on her lanai frequently appeared in the tabloids. Following his 2006 separation from Denise Richards, Charlie Sheen also took refuge here.

11. OCEANA HOTEL, 849 Ocean Ave.

Stan Laurel (of "Laurel and Hardy") died here in 1965. Laurel spent his last years living at the hotel.

(Note: To reach the following two properties, backtrack on Ocean Avenue and turn right on California Avenue incline, which will take you down to Pacific Coast Highway. California is one block north of Wilshire Boulevard.

A word of caution: Unless you park, you cannot sightsee on Palisades Beach Road—or Pacific Coast Highway—because there is always too much traffic.)

12. PETER LAWFORD'S BEACH HOUSE, 625 Palisades Beach Road (Note: Palisades Beach Road is what Pacific Coast Highway is called beneath Santa Monica's bluffs)

Once film mogul Louis B. Mayer's Santa Monica beach house, this mansion was later owned by actor Peter

Lawford and his wife Pat, one of John F. Kennedy's sisters. In *Peter Lawford: The Man Who Kept The Secrets,* author James Spada wrote: "For the first two years of the Kennedy administration, Pat and Peter's beach years of the Kennedy administration, Pat and Peter's beach house was essentially the Western White House. Officially, the President stayed at the Beverly Hilton Hotel, but he spent his days relaxing by his sister and brother-in-law's pool . . . When he was at Peter Lawford's house, he was there to relax and have a good time—and Peter saw to it that he did. Whenever Jack visited when Pat was away, Peter could be counted on to throw a party for him that included, in addition to Peter's show business friends, lovely young starlets, models—and hookers. After an evening of partying, Jack would choose one or two of the prettiest to return with them to his hotel suite. Some of the parties at Lawford's house—those peopled by a great many legendary beautiful women and a great many older married men—became legendary." Lawford's next-door neighbor told author Anthony Summers: "it was nothing but La Dolce Vita over there. It was like a goddamn whorehouse.' And Jack Kennedy hustled his wife. He wanted her to go to Hawaii with him. 'It was the most disgusting thing I've ever seen.'"

13. 415 PCH BEACH CLUB, 415 Palisades Beach Road
This public beach club has an intriguing history. On the site once stood an 118-room, 55-bath mansion that newspaper magnate William Randolph Hearst built in 1928 for his mistress, actress Marion Davies, for a then unheard-of cost of $7 million. Producer Richard Zanuck, who grew up down the street, once remarked: "It made *Gone With the Wind's* Tara look like a guesthouse."
The main house was torn down in 1955, but the servants' wings became part of an exclusive private beach club, the Sand and Sea Club. When the Sand and Sea closed

in 1991, the state leased the property for filming—and "Beverly Hills 90210" used the beach club as a focal point for its summer shows.

Now, anyone can park next door, have lunch, and walk, bike or rollerblade on the boardwalk past the club and the beachfront houses of a number of Hollywood legends. These include Harold Lloyd's getaway at 443 Palisades Beach Road, Mae West's at 514, Twentieth-Century Fox head Darryl Zanuck's at 546, Samuel Goldwyn's at 602, Harry Warner's two homes at 605 and 607, Louis B. Mayer and later Peter Lawford's at 625, Douglas Fairbanks and Mary Pickford's at 705, and MGM production chief Irving Thalberg and silent screen star Norma Shearer's at 707.

About a mile down the street, a beach house at 1038 Palisades Beach Road is famous because it was variously lived in by Norma Talmadge; Cary Grant, first with his roommate, Randolph Scott, and then his wife, Barbara Hutton; Princess Grace Kelly; and actress Sharon Tate and her husband, director Roman Polanski.

14. FORMER JANE FONDA HOUSE, 316 Alta Drive

Fonda lived here before she married Ted Turner in 1991.

15. PATRICK'S ROADHOUSE, 106 Entrada Dr. (at Pacific Coast Highway), (310) 459-4544

Notorious celebrity hangout.

16. LIFEGUARD STATION, TEMESCAL CANYON AND PACIFIC COAST HIGHWAY, around 16000 Pacific Coast Highway

At the height of its popularity "Baywatch" was the most watched television show on the planet, with an estimated one billion viewers in 144 countries. For nine years, beginning in 1989, David Hasselhoff oversaw the lifeguards at this lifeguard station, which was used for both exterior and interior shots. The station is located at Will Rogers State Beach.

NOT ON THE MAP is the Venice Pier, located at the end of Washington Boulevard in Venice. The pier was the site of the climactic scene in *Falling Down* (1993), in which Robert Duvall killed an out-of-control Michael Douglas.

The house that Eddie Murphy, Judge Reinhold, and John Ashton stormed in *Beverly Hills Cop* (1984)— supposedly in Beverly Hills—is actually at 609 W. Channel Road in Santa Monica Canyon.

SANTA MONICA is also home to directors Mel Brooks, Oliver Stone, Wes Craven, and Roger Corman; singer-songwriter Randy Newman; as well as radio hsot Leeza Gibbons and actors Marcia Cross, Blythe Danner, Dana Delaney, Peter Gallagher, Heather Graham, Marg Helgenberger and Alan Rosenberg, Barbara Hershey, Bonnie Hunt, Christine Lahti, Ving Rhames, and two of the Wilson brothers: Luke and Owen.

Former residents include Shirley Temple, whose first home was at 948 24th Street; and Kevin Spacey, who grew up at Fourth Street and Santa Monica Boulevards, in an area that seems to be rebuilt.

Dylan McDermott, former star of "The Practice," met his wife Ashar at the Novel Café at 212 Pier Avenue. Other former residents include Jeff Bridges, who lived at 436 Adelaide Drive; and writer Michael Crichton, who lived on La Mesa Drive.

CULVER CITY

1. SONY PICTURES STUDIOS, 10202 W. Washington Boulevard

Since 1991 this lot has been the home of Sony Pictures Studios, the parent company of Columbia Pictures. Before that (between 1924 and 1987), it was occupied by MGM, which was once considered to be Hollywood's leading studio.

Sony now offers a walking tour of the historic lot: it takes visitors to the sound stages where *The Wizard of Oz* (1939) and other musicals were scored; the historic Irving Thalberg Building, which houses the studios' Oscars; the studio wardrobe department; and sets where current feature films and television shows such as "Jeopardy" are filmed. Visitors aged 12 and over are welcome. The tour meets Mondays through Fridays four times a day in the lobby of Sony Pictures Plaza. Free parking is available under the plaza building on Madison Avenue, the side street between Washington and Culver boulevards. For hours and additional information call (323) 520-TOUR.

2. CULVER HOTEL, 9400 Culver Boulevard, (310) 838-7963

In 1938 most of the Munchkins stayed in this historic triangular-shaped hotel during the filming of *The Wizard of Oz* (1939). There is no truth to the claims the Munchkins held drunken orgies here. The hotel was once owned by John Wayne.

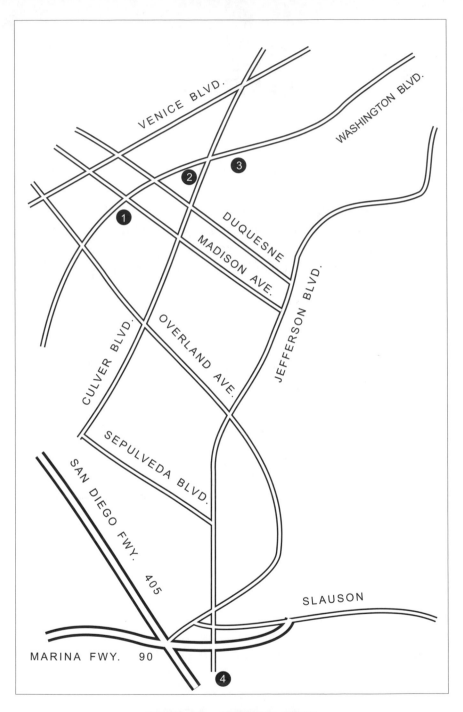

MAP 14 CULVER CITY

3. THE CULVER STUDIOS, 9336 Washington Boulevard

Owned by Sony Pictures and often rented out to other studios, the Culver Studios is the most interesting studio in Culver City to drive by. Its main attraction is the neo-colonial white mansion seen in the opening credits of all the David O. Selznick movies, including *Gone With the Wind* (1939). The burning of Atlanta and other scenes from the movie were filmed on the back lot along Ballona Creek, but the site is now an industrial tract.

Selznick, who also produced *King Kong* (1933) and the original *A Star is Born* (1937), was one of many to own the studio. Others include movie pioneer Thomas Ince, Cecil B. DeMille, RKO-Pathe, Desilu, Laird International Studios and Grant Tinker.

Interior shots for *E.T., City Slickers, What Women Want, Amagedon, Stuart Little,* and *Contact* were filmed here. The set for the Montecito Casino in the NBC dramedy "Las Vegas" was also built here.

Visitors are not allowed.

4. HILLSIDE CEMETERY, 6001 Centinela Avenue

When you drive on the San Diego Freeway between the airport and the West L.A., you cannot miss the six-column marble shrine to Al Jolson, who appeared in *The Jazz Singer* (1927), the first motion picture with synchronized sound. The memorial depicts him down on one knee, singing with his arms outstretched.

Jack Benny and Mary Livingstone Benny, Milton Berle, Eddie Cantor, David Janssen, George A. Jessel, Vic Morrow, hippe-turned-yuppie Jerry Rubin, Allan Sherman, and Aaron Spelling are also entombed at Hillside. So are crooners Percy Faith and Mel Torme.

Culver Studios.

The Sony Studios tour.

WESTWOOD AND
CENTURY CITY

1. DEAD MAN'S CURVE, Sunset Boulevard (across from the UCLA sports field)

Many people believed that "Dead Man's Curve," immortalized in song by Jan and Dean, referred to one of the curves on Mulholland Drive. Others believed it referred to a curve on Whittier Boulevard, by Buddy Hackett's house, where Jan Berry, one of the songwriters, was involved in a near-fatal car crash. (That accident actually happened after the song was released.) In *The L.A. Musical History Tour,* Art Fein reports that both Jan and Dean and co-writer Roger Christian agree "Dead Man's Curve" referred to a particularly curvy stretch of Sunset Boulevard across from the UCLA football field. Though most of Sunset Boulevard around UCLA and Beverly Hills remains curvy, Dead Man's Curve no longer exists. According to Fein, it was regraded after comedian Mel Blanc suffered a near-fatal crash there.

(Note: The chase scenes from 1984's *Against All Odds* were filmed on Sunset between Veteran Avenue and Beverly Glen Boulevard.)

2. UCLA, 405 Hilgard Avenue

UCLA boasts one of the finest film schools in the country. UCLA alumni in the arts include Jim Morrison, who, contrary to the impression left in Oliver Stone's *The Doors* (1991), was actually graduated with honors; Carol

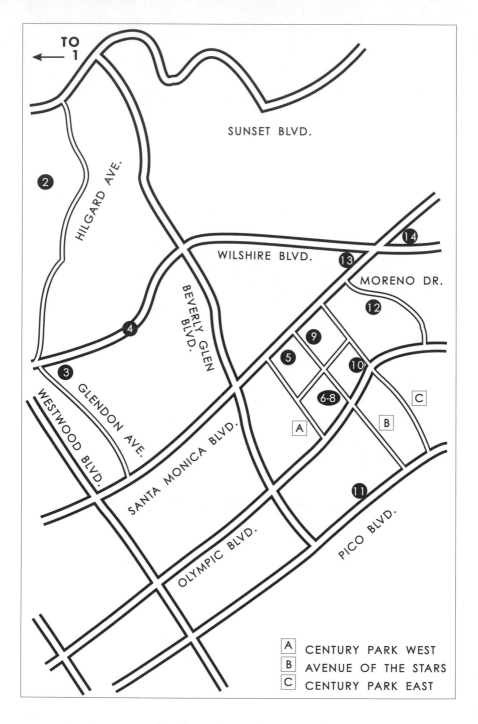

MAP 15 WESTWOOD & CENTURY CITY

Ovitz; *Doors* (1991), was actually graduated with honors; actors Carol Burnett; James Dean; Mark Harmon; Tim Robbins; directors Francis Ford Coppola and Alexander Payne, and conductor John Williams.

Catherine Bell, Jack Black, Jorge Garcia ("Hurley" on "Lost"), Brad Garrett, Heather Graham, Mariska Hargitay, Helen Hunt, Heather Locklear (whose father was once dean of UCLA's School of Engineering), Rob Reiner, and Ben Stiller are among UCLA's more famous dropouts.

UCLA is also a frequent location site. The 1996 remake of *The Nutty Professor*, starring Eddie Murphy, its sequel, *The Nutty Professor II* (2000), and *Gotcha!* (1985), starring Anthony Edwards, were filmed extensively on campus. So were many scenes from Reiner's *The Sure Thing* (1985). UCLA has also appeared in *Legally Blonde, Old School, Erin Brockovich, National Lampoon's Van Wilder, Mr. Baseball, Threesome*, and hundreds of commercials and television shows. In ABC's spy thriller "Alias" (2001-2006) this is where Jennifer Garner (as Syndey Bristow) attended college during the show's first two years.

3. WESTWOOD VILLAGE MEMORIAL PARK AND MORTUARY, 1218 Glendon Avenue

The cemetery, which is a little difficult to find (the driveway entrance is tucked away between an office building at the southeast corner of Wilshire Boulevard and a parking structure), attracts tourists who wish to pay their respects to Marilyn Monroe. Someday Marilyn will be kept company by Hugh Hefner, who bought the crypt adjacent to hers. Hefner paid $125,000 for the privilege of spending eternity next to the woman who launched his *Playboy* empire. In a romantic gesture, Hefner also bought an

The anniversary of Marilyn Monroe's death still brings out fans.

A view of Century City, including the Century Plaza Towers (center), Fox Plaza, where *Die Hard* was filmed (right), and 20th Century Fox (bottom right).

adjoining crypt for his estranged wife (but his seven girlfriends will not be joining them).

Near Marilyn's crypt, which is located in the Corridors of Memories, are the graves of two of the children from the *Poltergeist* movies (Dominique Dunne, who was strangled by her boyfriend; and Heather "They're here" O'Rourke, who died of a rare intestinal deformity at the age of 12); Dean Martin; 1980 *Playboy* Playmate of the Year Dorothy Stratten, whose story was memorialized in the chilling *Star 80* (1983); Twentieth-Century Fox production chief Darryl F. Zanuck; historians Will and Ariel Durant; Natalie Wood; Donna Reed; Truman Capote; Jack Lemmon; Walter Matthau; Buddy Rich; Roy Orbison; Robert Stack; and Rodney Dangerfield.

Peter Lawford was buried here, but his last wife Patty removed Lawford's ashes when cemetary officials insisted Lawford's crypt be fully paid for. According to James Spada, author of *Peter Lawford: The Man Who Kept the Secrets,* when Lawford was evicted from the cemetery, Patty made a deal with the *National Enquirer* "giving the tabloid exclusive picture rights in exchange for the limousine to take her to Marina del Rey, and a boat which to scatter Peter's ashes in the Pacific . . . Newspapers around the country told the story of Peter Lawford's last great indignity—his eviction from his final resting place."

4. JERRY RUBIN VERSUS A CAR, on Wilshire Boulevard, just west of Selby Avenue

This is the site where notorious 1960s yippie-turned-yuppie Jerry Rubin was struck by a car while jaywalking across Wilshire Boulevard. Rubin later died of internal injuries at UCLA Medical Center.

5. CENTURY CITY SHOPPING CENTER & MARKETPLACE, 10250 Santa Monica Boulevard, (310) 277-3898

6. CENTURY PLAZA HOTEL, 2025 Avenue of the Stars
One of Los Angeles' premier hotels, the Hyatt Regency Century Plaza is a frequent site of celebrity fundraisers. In 1972 Marilyn McCoo and Billy Davis, Jr., of the Fifth Dimension, were married behind the hotel and flew up, up and away in a hot air balloon.

7. PARK HYATT LOS ANGELES, 2151 Avenue of the Stars (at Galaxy Way), (310) 277-2777
In *Lethal Weapon 2* (1989) Mel Gibson and Danny Glover guarded Joe Pesci in the presidential suite of the Park Hyatt, and their stuntmen jumped into the swimming pool.
Also filmed here were the scenes in *Pacific Heights* (1990) in which Melanie Griffith, investigating Michael Keaton, tracked him to a room at the hotel. In *Point of No Return* (1993), Bridget Fonda planted a bomb, which destroyed part of the hotel.

8. FOX PLAZA, 2121 Avenue of the Stars
Located just yards from the back gate of 20th Century Fox, this is the building used as the site of the Nakatomi Corporation in *Die Hard* (1988). Bruce Willis tried to rescue hostages taken in the 33rd and 34th floors of the building, which was chosen for its high-tech look. Ironically, the building, owned by Fox at the time of the filming, was later sold to a Japanese concern.
Ronald Reagan also had his postpresidential offices here.

9. OFFICE BUILDING AT 1901 AVENUE OF THE STARS

In the bank robbery comedy *Bandits* (2001), Bruce Willis and Billy Bob Thornton held up a fictitious Alamo Savings & Loan supposedly located in this building.

10. CENTURY PLAZA TOWERS, 2029 and 2049 Century Park East

These twin office towers were depicted as the location of Cybill Shepherd and Bruce Willis' Blue Moon Detective Agency in "Moonlighting," and Stephanie Zimbalist and Pierce Brosnan's Steele Investigations in "Remington Steele."

11. TWENTIETH CENTURY FOX, 10201 W. Pico Boulevard

Unfortunately, Fox does not offer public tours, and virtually the only way to catch a glimpse of its back lot is to get tickets for one of the shows filming on the lot from one of the audience service companies. The studio has been located here since 1930.

12. BEVERLY HILLS HIGH SCHOOL, 241 S. Moreno Drive, Beverly Hills

Tourists sometimes drive past Beverly Hills High School thinking they will see the fictional West Beverly High in the television series "Beverly Hills 90210." Actually, the producers used Torrance High School in the Los Angeles suburb of Torrance, where filming permit costs are about one-fourth of what the city of Beverly Hills charges. Beverly Hills High School is still of interest, though, since it is one of the best high schools in the country. Its celebrity graduates include Corbin Bernsen, Albert Brooks, Nicolas Cage, Shaun and Patrick Cassidy,

Richard Chamberlain, Jamie Lee Curtis, Barry Diller, Richard Dreyfuss, Nora Ephron, Carrie and Joely Fisher, Rhonda Fleming, Bonnie Franklin, Gina Gershon, Joel Grey, Crispin Glover, Julie Kavner, Lenny Kravitz, Penny Marshall, Phil Morris, Laraine Newman, Rain Pryor, Rob Reiner, David Schwimmer, Pauly Shore, Jonathan Silverman, Alicia Silverstone, Marlo Thomas, Burt Ward, Betty White, and Kelli Williams.

It's a Wonderful Life (1946) was filmed on campus and there is a scene in the movie in which Jimmy Stewart and Donna Reed fell into the swimming pool there. The school was also lampooned in the feature film, *The Beverly Hillbillies* (1993).

13. BEVERLY HILTON HOTEL, 9876 Wilshire Boulevard, (310) 274-7777

The first Grammy Awards ceremonies were held at this hotel. In recent years the hotel has hosted the Golden Globe Awards and numerous celebrity fundraisers.

Richard Nixon made his famous "you-won't-have-Nixon-to-kick around-anymore" speech here after losing the 1962 California gubernatorial election.

14. PENINSULA BEVERLY HILLS HOTEL, 9882 Santa Monica Boulevard

The hotel is one of the highest-rated hotels in the city. Many actors dine or stay at the hotel, making it one of the best places for celebrity watchers. One actor—Jerry Seinfeld—joked to a reporter: "Let's go see the prostitutes in the bar."

NOT ON THE MAP—at 10355 Cheviot Drive, in the Cheviot Hills section of West Los Angeles—is the home depicted as Sela Ward's Chicago home during the first two seasons of the ABC family drama "Once and Again."

THE SUNSET STRIP

This is mostly a walking tour of what is often called "Hollywood's playground": the Sunset Strip. This tour also includes a few homes in the hills north of the Strip that are best reached by car. Most of the sites in this tour are within the city limits of West Hollywood. The dividing line between Los Angeles and West Hollywood is Sunset Boulevard; anything north of the Boulevard or east of the Chateau Marmont is within Los Angeles city limits.

Sites south of Sunset Boulevard are included in the West Hollywood section. Those who walk the Strip should keep in mind that a few sites listed in the West Hollywood section, including the apartment where Sal Mineo was stabbed to death and the apartment where Judith Campbell Exner lived when she had her affair with JFK, are within one or two blocks of Sunset Boulevard.

1. FORMER SITE OF SCHWAB'S PHARMACY, 8024 Sunset Boulevard (southeast corner of Crescent Heights)

Schwab's was the most famous drugstore in America, partly because its owner, pharmacist Leon Schwab, kept claiming that Lana Turner was "discovered" sitting on a stool at the soda fountain in his store. Turner herself has said on several occasions that there is no truth to the story, and it appears the tale was concocted by Schwab to lure customers to the store.

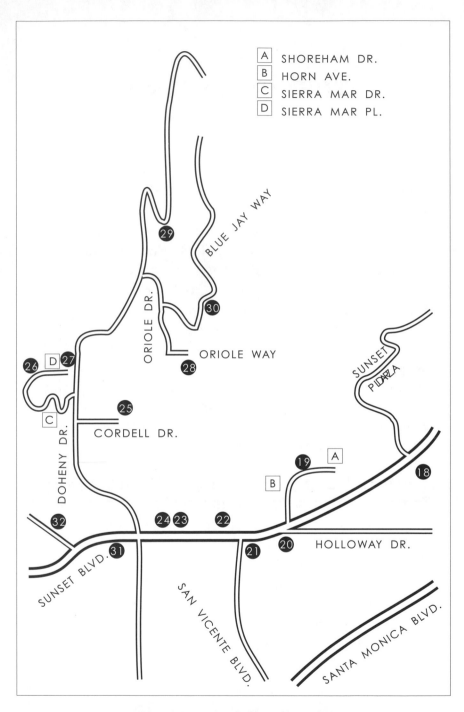

MAP 17 THE SUNSET STRIP

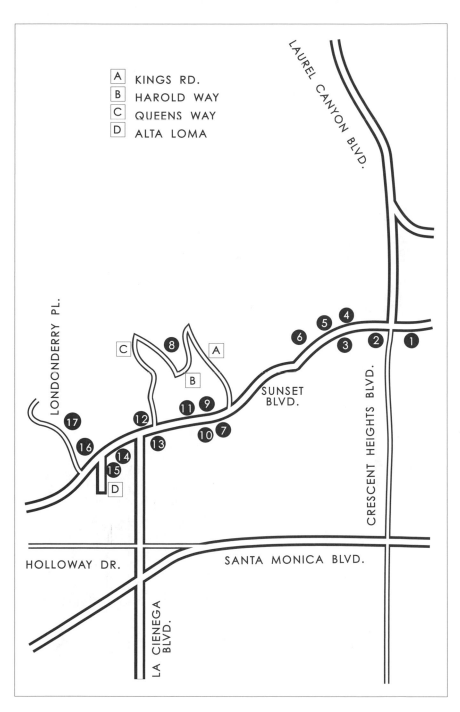

MAP 16   THE SUNSET STRIP

The moose and the squirrel were originally built to salute a sign across the street advertising a Las Vegas hotel. The sign featured a skimpily dressed Vegas showgirl.

A view of the Strip with the Santa Monica Mountains in the background.

There is, at least, truth to the story that in its heyday Schwab's was a popular hangout for writers and actors looking for work. In *Sunset Boulevard* (1950), William Holden called it "a combination office, coffee klatch and waiting room." Schwab filled prescriptions for studio executives and claimed he told them about some of the young budding actors who he thought were star material.

While Lana Turner was not discovered there, one regular, author F. Scott Fitzgerald, did have a heart attack there while buying cigarettes. Also, Graham Nash of Crosby, Stills & Nash met his wife there. The pharmacy was torn down in 1988 to make room for a block-long shopping complex anchored by Virgin Records.

2. FORMER SITE OF THE GARDEN OF ALLAH, 8152 Sunset Boulevard

Remember the song "Big Yellow Taxi," in which Joni Mitchell sang about paving paradise and putting up a parking lot? That was a reference to the tearing down of the Garden of Allah, another famous Hollywood landmark which once stood on the southwest corner of Sunset and Crescent Heights, directly across the street from Schwab's. The apartment/hotel was what one writer called the unofficial epicenter of Hollywood social activity during the 1930s and 1940s, with Frank Sinatra, Ava Gardner, Clark Gable, David Niven, Errol Flynn, the Marx Brothers, Robert Benchley, F. Scott Fitzgerald, Tallulah Bankhead, Clara Bow, Humphrey Bogart, Ernest Hemingway, and Leopold Stokowski among the major celebrities who were Garden residents at one time or another.

According to Bruce Torrence, author of *Hollywood: The First 100 Years:* "It was not uncommon to see tourists and movie fans lining the sidewalk just to get a glimpse of their favorite star." Torrence called the Garden's inhabitants "a fast-living, hard-drinking, high-rolling lot who burned

The Chateau Marmont.

The coroner's van and the media circus outside the Chateau Marmont on the day John Belushi died of a drug overdose.

out fast and took the Garden with them." In 1950 the Garden was sold to Lytton Savings and Loan, which tore it down and built its home office at the site. The site is now a minimall and a branch of Great Western Bank.

3. "ROCKY AND BULLWINKLE" STATUE, 8218 Sunset Boulevard

This converted house, once owned by Fess Parker, TV's "Davy Crockett," was for years the offices of Jay Ward Productions, the animation company that created "Rocky and Bullwinkle." A 15-foot-tall plaster statue of the famous moose and squirrel still stands in front of the building, as does a small courtyard which bears signatures of June Foray (the voices of both Rocky and Natasha) and, strangely enough, the elbowprints of the cartoon's writers.

The building is now owned by Hollywood Hounds, a doggie day center which offers doggie shiatsu massages, "pawdicures," and even "muttrimonies" and "bark mitzvahs."

4. CHATEAU MARMONT, 8221 Sunset Boulevard, (323) 656-1010

When celebrities visiting Los Angeles want to be seen, they often go to the Beverly Hills Hotel. When they wish to keep out of the limelight they often stay at the Marmont.

In his book *Life at the Marmont*, former owner Raymond L. Sarlot noted that the Marmont remains "one of [Hollywood's] best kept secrets, much to the joy of its celebrated clientele. Not too many years ago a *Newsday* journalist cornered Jill Clayburgh sipping coffee at [the hotel's coffee shop]. Following the usual career questions, she was asked to comment about her stay at the Marmont. 'Oh, don't mention the hotel,' she said, crinkling her face. 'Then all the tourists will come.' A moment later, Clayburgh was on her way, but not before leaving the journalist with a

Johnny Depp's castle. His living room reportedly features an electric chair and a dummy awaiting execution.

Christina Aguilera's home above the Sunset Strip.

final thought. 'If you must say something about this place, say it's terrible. Please say it's terrible.'"

The fact that tourists rarely discover the hotel is one of the reasons why stars like Marilyn Monroe, Nicole Kidman, Robert DeNiro, Josh Hartnett, Scarlet Johansson, Lindsay Lohan, Warren Beatty, Dustin Hoffman, John Lennon and Yoko Ono, Ringo Starr, Bob Dylan, Mick Jagger, Greta Garbo, Keanu Reeves, Leonardo DiCaprio, Matthew McConaughey, Sarah Jessica Parker, and the Eagles have all stayed for extended periods.

One former guest, John Belushi, did attract crowds when he died of a drug overdose on March 4, 1982, in bungalow 3. Several tabloids also claimed that Lindsay Lohan, who lived here almost for a year, overdosed on a dangerous cocktail of drugs on November 12, 2006.

In the movie *The Doors* (1991), Val Kilmer, playing Jim Morrison, was seen trying to leap out of a sixth-floor penthouse. The Righteous Brothers song "You've Lost That Lovin' Feelin'" was reportedly written at the hotel. According to published reports, the hotel places screenplays in its night stands instead of Bibles.

5. CABO CANTINA, 8301 Sunset Boulevard (at Sweetzer), (323) 656-6388

This restaurant was formerly the Source, the natural foods restaurant where Diane Keaton dumped Woody Allen in *Annie Hall* (1977).

6. MANSION OWNED BY JOHNNY DEPP (high on the hillside just west of Sweetzer Avenue)

When actor Johnny Depp bought this 29-room mansion in 1995, some entertainment magazines reported that it was once owned by Bela Lugosi and that the Munchkins stayed there during the filming of *The Wizard of Oz* (1939). Hollywood historian Laurie Jacobson insists that neither claim is correct, and that the castle only *looks* like the type of home the one-time *Dracula* star might have lived in.

In fact, the castle was once owned by Hersee Moody Carson, the childless widow of a multimillionaire, and it was called the "Castle of the Fairy Lady" because she used to hold parties there for orphans on major holidays during the 1930s and 1940s. Before Depp shelled out $2.3 million for the gated estate, it was owned by divorce attorney Michael Mitchelson, who lost it in a bankruptcy after being convicted of tax fraud.

What you can see from Sunset, behind thick foliage, is the backside of the mansion. The front entrance is on North Sweetzer Avenue.

The art deco Sunset Tower Hotel has been a Hollywood hot spot for more than half a century.

7. SUNSET TOWER, 8358 Sunset Boulevard, (323) 654-7100

This luxury hotel was once the home to Hollywood stars such as John Wayne, Marilyn Monroe, Clark Gable, Errol Flynn, Howard Hughes, Roger Moore, Truman Capote, and the Gabor sisters. One resident, Bugsy Siegel, was reportedly asked to leave after he was arrested for placing bets at the hotel.

The building itself is an intriguing 13-story Art Deco tower emblazoned with mythological creatures, zeppelins, airplanes, and Adam and Eve.

The hotel is occasionally used as a film location and has served as the outside of the Voltaire Restaurant in *Pretty Woman* (1990), John Travolta's hotel in *Get Shorty* (1995), and the site of Jamie Lee Curtis' wedding rehearsal in the 2003 remake of *Freaky Friday*. In the Hollywood satire *The Player* (1992), Tim Robbins was pitched a story idea by the hotel's rooftop pool. In *The Italian Job* (2003), Mark Wahlberg, Charlize Theron, and their fellow thieves rendezvoused here while plotting to resteal gold they originally stole in Venice, only to be doublecrossed by Ed Norton.

8. LIBERACE HOME, 8433 Harold Way (between Kings and Queens Road)

Liberace lived in this 28-room mansion from 1961 to 1979. He told his biographer Bob Thomas, author of *Liberace*: "I tried to turn this place into a museum. In one month we had seventeen thousand reservations. But the neighbors complained" about traffic from the tourists. Liberace's museum was instead built in Las Vegas.

9. HYATT WEST HOLLYWOOD ON SUNSET, 8401 Sunset Boulevard (at Kings Road), (323) 656-4101

In the 1960s and 1970s, when the hotel was the Continental Hyatt House, and a favorite of rock and rollers, the hotel was better known as "The Riot House." According to Art Fein's *L.A. Musical History Tour* book, "Led Zeppelin rented as many as six floors here for their carryings on. Their partying set a standard that has never been equaled, with orgies, motorcycles in the halls, and stories yet untold." Fein also reports that "The Rolling Stones movie *Cocksucker Blues* shows Keith Richards and Bobby Keyes throwing a television out a window of this hotel" and that the Doors' "Jim Morrison lived here until he was evicted by management for hanging out a window by his fingertips, dangling over the pavement." Little Richard lived here through much of the 1980s and 1990s.

10. HOUSE OF BLUES, 8430 Sunset Boulevard (at Olive), (323) 848-5100

Investors in this nightclub include Blues Brother Dan Aykroyd.

11. COMEDY STORE, 8433 Sunset Boulevard, (323) 656-6225

One of Los Angeles's premier comedy clubs, the Comedy Store has featured performances from every important comedian. The names of its headliners are vaunted on its outside walls. This was once the site of Ciro's, one of Hollywood's most popular nightclubs during the 1940s and 1950s.

The building is supposedly haunted. TV's "Access Hollywood" once brought in a psychic, billed her as a "spiritual journalist," and had her talk about angry mobsters still supposedly trapped in the building's basement.

12. PIAZZA DEL SOL, 8439 Sunset Boulevard

This Spanish Revival apartment building was designated a historic landmark because of its beauty, not because of its notorious history. During the 1930s, this was the site of Lee Francis' "House of Francis," the classiest brothel on the Sunset Strip. The building now houses the offices of several production companies—the names of which most people would not recognize. The brothels are now located in private homes above the Strip.

13. MONDRIAN HOTEL, 8440 Sunset Boulevard (at Queens Road), (323) 650-8999

This classy hotel caters to celebrities in the music, entertainment, and fashion industries. Members of Guns and Roses, The Who, Hole (including Courtney Love), the Smashing Pumpkins, the Cranberries, Public Enemy, Gipsy Kings, and Poison have stayed here, as have many actors. In *Doc Hollywood* (1991), Michael J. Fox stayed in room 1110. The hotel's nightclub, "Sky Bar," which provides panoramic views of the city, is so popular that hotel employees refer to it as "celebrity central."

14. SITE OF "77 SUNSET STRIP," 8532 Sunset Boulevard

Although fans of the popular 1950s TV series would never recognize it today, the front door of the Tiffany Theater is where Efrem Zimbalist, Jr., and Roger Smith played private eyes at the fictitious address "77 Sunset Strip."

The restaurant next to their offices, Dino's Lodge—which was once owned by Dean Martin—is also gone. It has been replaced by an office building housing Casablanca Records. Fans of the show will remember Edd "Kookie" Byrnes parking cars at Dino's Lodge.

15. SUNSET MARQUIS HOTEL AND VILLAS, 1200 N. Alta Loma Road

The Marquis has its own recording studio, making it a long-time favorite of recording artists. Aerosmith, the Rolling Stones, Hall & Oates, Ozzy Osbourne, and Dave Matthews are among the musicians who have stayed and recorded there.

Sunset Plaza is another great place for people-watching.

When the *Playboy* building was next door, *Playboy* executives would bring the bunnies here for afternoon dalliances.

The hotel's Bar 1200 (formerly the Whisky Bar) is a long-time Hollywood hangout.

16. APARTMENT AT 1326 LONDONDERRY VIEW
(one block north of Sunset, off Londonderry Place)

Jane Wyman lived in apartment 5 here in the late 1930s, just three blocks from Ronald Reagan's house at 1128 Cory Avenue. After they married on January 26, 1940, Reagan moved in with her. However, the apartment proved to be too small after their first daughter, Maureen, was born, and the Reagans built a house at nearby 9137 Cordell Drive (covered later on the tour, page 129).

17. FORMER HOME OF DAVID SCHWIMMER, 1330
Londonderry Place

Schwimmer lived in this traditional-style home when he starred on NBC's "Friends." In 2001 he moved to a larger $5.5 million home in Hancock Park.

18. SUNSET PLAZA

This is a two-block cluster of hip outdoor cafes, boutiques, hair salons, and other stores whose prices rival those of Rodeo Drive's. It is one of the best people-watching places in town.

19. SHOREHAM TOWERS, 8787 Shoreham Drive (at Horn)

David Lee Roth and Neil Sedaka are among the many celebrities who have lived in this condominium complex. A house that Humphrey Bogart shared with Mayo Method, his second wife (and the one who stabbed him), once stood on this site.

In 1969, Art Linkletter's daughter Diane jumped to her death from a sixth-floor apartment here after taking LSD. In 1995, another tragedy occurred when ballet star turned actor Alexander Godunov died in his condo of alcohol abuse.

20. BOOK SOUP, 8818 Sunset Boulevard

This independent bookstore caters to the entertainment industry and does quite a few celebrity signings, making it an excellent place for celebrity sighting.

Book Soup appeared in *Single White Female* (1992) as the store where Jennifer Jason Lee worked, and in 2005's *Bewitched*, where Will Farrell spotted Nicole Kidman wiggling her nose and tried to recruit her as his leading lady.

21. THE VIPER ROOM, 8852 Sunset Boulevard

On October 31, 1993, 23-year-old River Phoenix died of a drug overdose outside this nightclub once owned by Johnny Depp.

Depp told an interviewer he named the club "after a group of musicians who called themselves Vipers. They were reefer heads and they helped start modern music."

In the 1940s, the club was known as the Melody Room and was a notorious hangout for Los Angeles mobsters.

22. THE WHISKY A GO GO, 8901 Sunset Boulevard (at Clark Street), (310) 652-4202

This was the West Coast's first discotheque. "Gogo" dancing was born here.

23. THE ROXY, 9009 Sunset Boulevard, (310) 276-2222

The Roxy is one of Los Angeles' top music clubs and showcases for new talent. Although nearby restaurants claim otherwise, John Belushi had his last supper here at On The Rox, an exclusive private club above the Roxy.

24. RAINBOW BAR AND GRILL, 9015 Sunset Boulevard, (323) 278-4232

Vincente Minnelli proposed to Judy Garland, and Marilyn Monroe met her future husband, Joe DiMaggio, on a blind date, when the Grill's predecessor, the Villa Nova Restaurant, was here.

25. HOUSE AT 9137 CORDELL DRIVE (north of Doheny Drive)

Ronald Reagan lived here with his first wife, Jane Wyman, from 1941 until their divorce in 1948. According to Anne Edwards' biography *Early Reagan*, he separated from Wyman several times during 1947 and 1948, and during two of those separations he moved into the Garden of Allah. After the house was sold, Reagan moved back to an apartment at 1326 Londonderry View.

26. FORMER JERRY SEINFELD HOME, 9444 Sierra Mar Place

Seinfeld lived in this gated, 6,000-square-foot mansion from 1992 to 1998, the years when his eponymous show, "Seinfeld," was the highest rated sitcom on television. The house, just off windy Sierra Mar Drive, was later sold to one of his executive producers, who in turn sold it to an unknown party who, according to neighbors, used to get visitors at all hours of the day and night, some leaving used condoms on the street.

The house was sold again for in 2004 for $5.1 million. Previous tenants included the Smothers Brothers, David Geffen, and actor George Montgomery, whose daughter Elizabeth was "Samantha" on TV's "Betwitched." The house is now inhabited by a real-life witch.

27. "DISNEY'S THE KID" HOUSE, 9405 Sierra Mar Place

Located a short stroll up the street Seinfeld's former house is a modernistic house that has been a frequent film location. This was Bruce Willis' house in the *Disney's The Kid* (2000). Three years after the movie filmed, the house's owner was brutally beaten to death here.

28. FORMER MADONNA HOME, 9045 Oriole Way

Madonna bought this gated three-bedroom house for $3 million in 1989 from Allen Questron, the former president and CEO of Neiman Marcus, and sold it for $2 million during California's 1994 real estate slump. Subsequent owners included Leonardo di Caprio.

29. HOUSE AT 1654 DOHENY DRIVE

This three-story Spanish house is famous for two reasons. According to her memoir *Madame 90210*, Hollywood madam Alex Adams operated a brothel here for several years before her 1988 arrest.

The house was subsequently rented by actress Shannen Doherty during the years she starred on "Beverly Hills 90210." According to a lawsuit filed by her former landlord, Doherty trashed the home and left in the dead of night owing $14,000 in overdue rent.

30. BLUE JAY WAY (side street off Oriole Drive)

In his book *L.A. Musical History Tour*, Art Fein reports that "George Harrison rented a house on this street in 1968, just before the Beatles recorded Magical Mystery Tour. Their publicist Derek Taylor had such difficulty finding the place in the fog one night that Harrison penned 'Blue Jay Way,' a dreamy paean to it, which emerged on that album. The street might still be hard to find, because residents report that the street sign is frequently stolen by Beatle(klepto)-maniacs."

31. "BIG SLEAZY" PRIVATE INVESTIGATIONS, 9200 Sunset Boulevard

Anthony Pellicano, the infamous private eye who earned the epithet "the Big Sleazy," long before the indictments kept coming, initially pled guilty to keeping an arsenal of hand grenades and illegal explosives in his office here in the Luckman Plaza. In 2006 Pellicano was indicted a second time on 112 different charges of wiretapping and witness tampering. Pellicano allegedly spied on Hollywood celebrities (and sometimes their wives) on behalf of his famous clients.

His clients included some of the biggest names in Hollywood, including former Creative Artists Agency head Michael Ovitz; manager-producer, and later Paramount Pictures head, Brad Grey; director John Tiernan (best known for *Die Hard* and *The Hunt for Red October),* who pled guilty to wiretapping; and $900-an-hour "superlawyer" Bert Fields. Fields and Pellicano worked hand in hand trying to discredit the family of the 13-year-old boy who originally accused Michael Jackson of child molestation. Fields also has been the chief defender of Tom Cruise's manhood and religion. A target of the federal grand jury investigation probing Pellicano, Fields evaded his own indictment when Pellicano refused to testify against him. While Pellicano's other employers distanced themselves from the disgraced P.I., Fields helped the embattled Pellicano financially by establishing a fund to support the education of Pellicano's children.

Pellicano, who cultivated his image as a tough, baseball-bat-wielding intimidator of opposing parties in lawsuits, was tied to a number of disturbing incidents and suspected of hiring thugs to terrify several members of the press. Anita Busch, a former *Los Angeles Times* reporter who was writing about actor Steven Segal, another Pellicano client, discovered a dead fish and a threatening note on her broken car windshield. Journalist-turned-director-and-producer Rod Lurie suspected that Pellicano arranged for Lurie to become a hit-and-run victim while he was bicycle riding. Pellicano suspiciously called him the following day to ask about his injuries. Similarly, Ned Zeman, a staff writer for *Vanity Fair* who was doing a separate piece on Segal, was threatened on a Laurel Canyon road when a dark Mercedes that had been following him pulled alongside his car. A man in the Mercedes pointed a pistol at Zeman and pulled the trigger. Instead of firing, however, the man said "Stop!" and then "Bang!" He was clearly trying to tell Zeman what might happen if he did not abandon the article.

As this book goes to press, Pellicano is awaiting trial.

32. SIERRA TOWERS, 9255 Doheny Drive

Paparazzi can often be seen milling outside this exclusive 32-story condominium, where tabloid headliners Matthew Perry, Cher, Elton John, and Kate Moss all own units.

Former residents include "Dragnet"'s Jack Webb, who lived and died here; Joan Collins, George Hamilton, David Janssen, Sidney Poitier, and jockey Bill Shoemaker. Lindsay Lohan bought a unit here, but never moved in.

Actor Peter Lawford also lived here in the late 1960s and early 1970s, after he sold his beach house in Santa Monica. Lawford moved out of Sierra Towers after the 6.4 earthquake that shook Los Angeles on February 9, 1971, reportedly because he did not like the way the building swayed in the quake.

(SIGHTSEEING NOTE: Tourists who wish to combine the Sunset Strip and Beverly Hills tours can do so by continuing west on Doheny. Hillcrest Drive—which is where the Beverly Hills tour in this book starts—is just two blocks west of Sierra Towers on Doheny. See page 19.)

QUITE A FEW CELEBRITIES own or have owned homes in the so-called bird streets north of the Strip—streets with names like Swallow, Robin, Oriole, Thrasher, and Blue Jay. Among them are Jennifer Aniston (who once rented her house to Sasha Baron Cohen and his fiancée, Isla Fisher), Jodi Foster, Tobey Maguire, Megan Mullally, Keanu Reeves, Winona Ryder, Tori Spelling, and Alan Thicke.

Other celebrities who own homes in the neighborhood include Halle Berry, Jim Brown, Herbie Hancock, Richard Lewis, Jon Lovitz, Johnny Mathis, Leslie Nielsen, and KISS's Gene Simmons.

Former residents include Courteney Cox, who, in the late 1980s, owned another home at 8815 Appian Way. This was the same home Carole King lived in when her 1971 album "Tapestry" was released.

WEST HOLLYWOOD

1. SITE OF SAL MINEO STABBING, 8569 Holloway Drive (one block south of Sunset Boulevard, between Alta Loma Road and Westmount Drive)

The 37-year-old actor, who is best known for his Academy Award-nominated performance in *Rebel Without a Cause* (1955), was stabbed to death on February 12, 1976, in the carport of this apartment building. Mineo lived next door at 8565 Holloway Drive.

2. MARILYN MONROE / SHELLEY WINTERS APARTMENT, 8575 Holloway Boulevard

Next door to Mineo's apartment, at what is now 8575 Holloway, is a separate apartment that Marilyn Monroe shared with Shelley Winters in the early 1950s. According to Winters' autobiography *Shelley: Also Known as Shirley,* Marilyn talked about how nice it would be "to be like men and just get notches on your belt" without getting emotionally involved. The two then made an extensive list of all the prominent men they wanted to sleep with. One of Marilyn's surprise picks was Albert Einstein.

3. LAST HOME OF DOROTHY DANDRIDGE (EL PALACIO APARTMENTS), 8495 Fountain Avenue

Actress-singer-dancer Dandridge, Hollywood's first black sex symbol, was often compared to Marilyn Monroe. After she was nominated for an Academy Award for *Carmen Jones* (1954), Dandridge's career sank and she

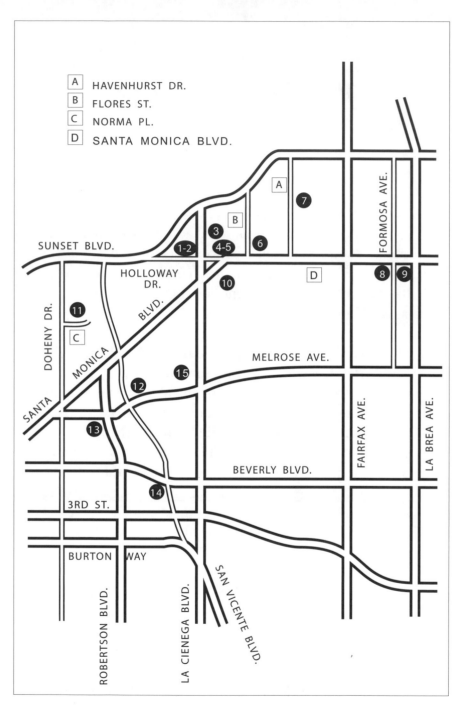

A HAVENHURST DR.
B FLORES ST.
C NORMA PL.
D SANTA MONICA BLVD.

SUNSET BLVD.

FORMOSA AVE.

A

B

HOLLOWAY DR.

HOLLOWAY BLVD.

SANTA MONICA

DOHENY DR.

C

D

MELROSE AVE.

FAIRFAX AVE.

LA BREA AVE.

BEVERLY BLVD.

3RD ST.

BURTON WAY

ROBERTSON BLVD.

LA CIENEGA BLVD.

SAN VICENTE BLVD.

MAP 18 WEST HOLLYWOOD

became another of Hollywood's tragedies. At the age of 39 she declared bankruptcy. Three years later she suffered the same fate as Monroe when she died from a pill-and-alcohol overdose. Halle Berry played her in the TV movie "Introducing Dorothy Dandridge."

4. BARNEY'S BEANERY, 8447 Santa Monica Boulevard, (323) 654-2287

This old-time diner, sometimes featured on TV's "Columbo" as Peter Falk's favorite eatery, was once frequented by musicians like Janis Joplin and Jim Morrison. It is still considered a rock 'n rollers' hangout.

Actors-turned-directors Penny Marshall and Rob Reiner met here in 1969. They subsequently divorced.

In 2003's conjoined twin comedy *Stuck on You*, it was here that Greg Kinnear told Matt Damon he wanted an operation to separate the two.

5. EMSER RUGS AND TILE, 8431 Santa Monica Boulevard (one block east of La Cienega Boulevard)

In the first *Lethal Weapon* (1985), a suicidal Mel Gibson tried to talk a suicidal man out of jumping off the building. When the man would not listen, Gibson went nuts and they both ended up taking a plunge off the building into an air bag.

6. FORMER APARTMENT OF JFK MISTRESS JUDITH CAMPBELL EXNER, 1200 N. Flores Street

Exner is the woman who was intimate with both President John F. Kennedy and mobster Sam Giancana during Kennedy's White House years, and who claimed to have aborted JFK's baby. She also claimed to have served as a courier between JFK and Giancana, carrying envelopes back and forth between them in 1960 and 1961. Although she claims she never peeked inside, she later suggested the envelopes carried payoffs intended to influence the 1960 presidential election. Frank Sinatra reportedly introduced Exner to JFK.

In 1961 Exner lived here, in apartment 201. In her autobiography *My Story*, she claimed she was harassed by FBI agents who learned of her affair with Kennedy, and in 1962 moved to another apartment at 8401 Fountain Avenue.

7. COLONIAL HOUSE, 1416 N. Havenhurst Drive

Julia Roberts, Jodie Foster, Sandra Bullock, Jennifer Lopez, Jamie Lee Curtis, Winona Ryder, Hugh Grant and Elizabeth Hurley, Ellen DeGeneres, Tim Burton, Bette Davis, Clark Gable and Carole Lombard, all lived in this French colonial condominium. So did Sammy Glick, the protagonist in Budd Schulberg's classic novel of Hollywood, *"What Makes Sammy Run?"*

8. THE LOT, 1041 Formosa Avenue

In the early 1920s, this was the Pickford-Fairbanks Studios, where Fairbanks made his classics *Robin Hood* (1922) and *The Thief of Baghdad* (1940). Later it became Goldwyn Studios, and between 1980 and 2000 it was owned by Warner Bros. and used for the production of both motion pictures and television programs. It is now an independent production lot. Quinn Martin's shows, "Barnaby Jones," "Cannon," and "The Fugitive," were all filmed here, as were "Love Boat," "Dynasty," and feature films such as *Austin Power in Goldmember, Volcano, Basic Instinct, Contact, The Majestic, Pay It Forward,* and *Species.* The studio's Goldwyn Sound Facilities, which provided the postproduction sound for *Star Wars, Raiders of the Lost Ark,* and the *Rocky* pictures, is arguably the most prestigious sound department in the business. No tours; visitors are not allowed.

9. FORMOSA CAFE, 7156 Santa Monica Boulevard, (323) 850-9050

This famed Chinese-American restaurant, a favorite of Hollywood hipsters, was once frequented by Marilyn Monroe, Humphrey Bogart, and Clark Gable. In *L.A. Confidential* (1997), police detectives investigating Lana Turner's mafia boyfriend mistook Turner for a hooker.

In real life, the Formosa was the scene of an infamous May 3, 1997, incident that almost derailed Eddie Murphy's career. The actor was stopped by police in the wee hours of the morning after he picked up a male transvestite prostitute. The police let Murphy go, and his publicist claimed Murphy was just being a good Samaritan for offering the transvestite a ride.

Murphy went on to make family films. The prostitute, however, was arrested and charged on outstanding warrants.

10. 24 HOUR FITNESS SPORT, 8612 Santa Monica Boulevard

This is the gym where the less-than-perfect John Travolta-Jamie Lee Curtis movie *Perfect* (1985) was filmed.

11. FORMER HOME OF DOROTHY PARKER, 8983 Norma Place

Humorist Dorothy Parker lived in this white stucco bungalow in the early 1960s; and it was here, on June 14, 1963, that she found her husband, Alan Campbell, dead. According to her biographer Leslie Frewin, in *The Late Mrs. Dorothy Parker*, a neighbor asked Parker: "Dottie, tell me, dear. What can I do to help you?" Parker answered: "Get me a new husband." When the neighbor said how appalled she was by Parker's remark, Parker reportedly made her famous remark: "Sorry. Then run down to the corner and get me a ham and cheese on rye and tell them to hold the mayo."

12. PACIFIC DESIGN CENTER, 8667 Melrose Avenue
Sometimes referred to as "The Blue Whale," the Design Center is the West Coast's largest resource for upscale residential and office furnishings The building is open to the public; however, purchases must be made through design professionals. The Whale was depicted as Sandra Bullock's home in *Demolition Man* (1993) starring Sylvester Stallone and Wesley Snipes.

13. CEDARS-SINAI MEDICAL CENTER, 8700 Beverly Boulevard (city of Los Angeles)
Hollywood's Grave Line Tour liked to point out that many celebrities (Frank Sinatra, Danny Kaye, Sammy Davis, Jr., Lucille Ball, Peter Lawford, Jack Warner, Barry White) died here. Of course, the reason so many stars die here is because it is one of finest hospitals in the country, and dying stars want the best. Madonna, Britney Spears, Jodi Foster, Jennifer Garner, Michelle Pfeiffer, Mary Hart, Ronald and Nancy Reagan, Michael J. Fox, Michael Jackson, Clint Eastwood, Pierce Brosnan, Warren Beatty and Annette Bening are among the dozens of celebrities who have had children delivered here.

14. BEVERLY CENTER, 8500 Beverly Boulevard at La Cienega Boulevard (city of Los Angeles)
In *Volcano* (1997), the lava flow that was about to engulf this upscale shopping center—and destroy L.A.'s westside —was rerouted when demolition crews blew up a

high-rise across the street. (The building was digitally imposed.)

The Woody Allen-Bette Midler feature *Scenes from a Mall* (1990) was supposed to have been set in the Beverly Center. However, with the exception of a few exterior scenes, most of the film was actually filmed at the Stamford Town Center in Stamford, Connecticut.

Scenes from *Selena* (1997) starring Jennifer Lopez also filmed here.

15. "WRONG DOOR RAID" APARTMENT, 8122 Waring Avenue, (corner of Kilkea Drive, north of Melrose Avenue and one block west of Crescent Heights Boulevard)

During his divorce proceedings with Marilyn Monroe, Joe DiMaggio wanted to prove she was having an affair with her acting coach. The baseball legend hired a detective, who reported that Monroe spent a lot of time in her friend's apartment on the corner of Kilkea and Waring. Suspecting that this was the site of a tryst, DiMaggio and his friend Frank Sinatra arranged for a thug to break into the apartment and start taking pictures. The only problem was they broke into the wrong apartment, and the thugs terrorized the 37-year-old woman next door. The woman subsequently sued the duo for $200,000 and settled out of court for $7,500.

NOT ON THE MAP is a house at 8723 Rangeley Avenue, where Dominique Dunne, who played the older sister in *Poltergeist* (1982), was strangled to death by her estranged boyfriend, John Sweeney. Sweeney served only four years in prison. The murder and Sweeney's early release inspired Dominique's father, producer-turned-gossip-columnist Dominick Dunne, to write books and articles railing against rich and famous people who commit murder.

A FEW RESTAURANTS IN AND NEAR WEST HOLLYWOOD WHERE YOU HAVE THE BEST CHANCE OF SEEING SOMEONE FAMOUS:

• THE IVY, 113. N. Robertson Boulevard, (310) 274-8303
    When stars feel the need to be photographed, they go to the restaurant's outdoor patio.

• AGO, 8478 Melrose Avenue, (323) 655-3333
    This is where director Quentin Tarantino punched an author, slamming him into a wall. Tarantino, whose cinematic blood baths are almost like ballets, claimed he just "bitch-slapped" the poor scribe.

• KOI, 730 N. La Cienega Blvd.
    Scene of several paparazzi incidents.

• DAN TANA'S, 9071 Santa Monica Boulevard, (310) 275-9444
    Producer Aaron Spelling named Robert Urich's character in "Vega$" after the restaurant's owner.

• MORTON'S, 8800 Melrose Avenue, (310) 276-1253
    Studio heads, superagents and their biggest stars often did business over dinner here. Morton's is also where Kim Basinger and Alec Baldwin had their first date, and Ellen DeGeneres first eyed Anne Heche at the 1997 Academy Awards party hosted by *Vanity Fair*.
    In 2008 Morton's closed its doors and became Soho House, a members-only social club.

HOLLYWOOD

1. HOLLYWOOD HERITAGE MUSEUM, 2100 N. Highland Avenue

Dedicated to early Hollywood filmmaking, the Hollywood Heritage Museum is located in the barn where Cecil B. DeMille directed *The Squaw Man,* the first nationally successful feature-length film shot in Hollywood. The movie's success inspired other filmmakers to follow the lead of DeMille and producer Jesse Lasky and set up shop in Hollywood. Paramount Studios' original studio lot developed around the barn.

The barn, which was originally located a few miles east of its present site—at the intersection of Selma and Vine Streets—was subsequently moved to Paramount's current back lot on Melrose Avenue, where it was used as the railroad station in "Bonanza." The barn was later donated by Paramount Pictures and the Hollywood Chamber of Commerce to Hollywood Heritage, Inc., which operates the museum.

Hours vary during the year. Call (323) 874-2276 for further information.

2. HOLLYWOOD BOWL, 2301 N. Highland Avenue

Since its opening in 1922, this world-famous outdoor amphitheater has hosted performances by virtually every well-known musician.

The Bowl Museum is open daily; call (323) 850-2058 for hours. There is no charge for admission.

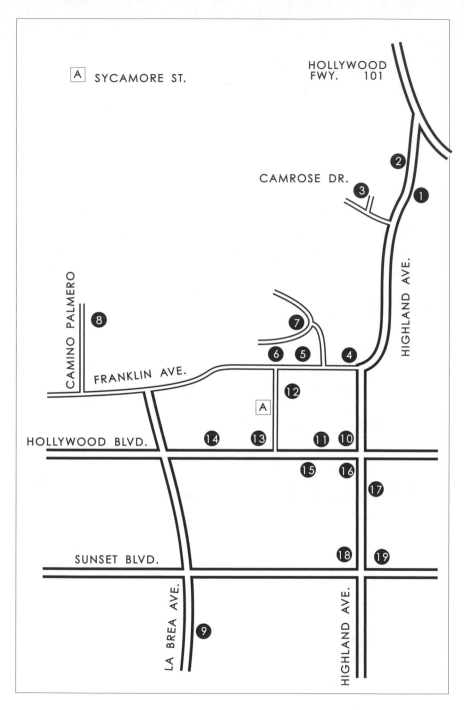

MAP 19 HOLLYWOOD

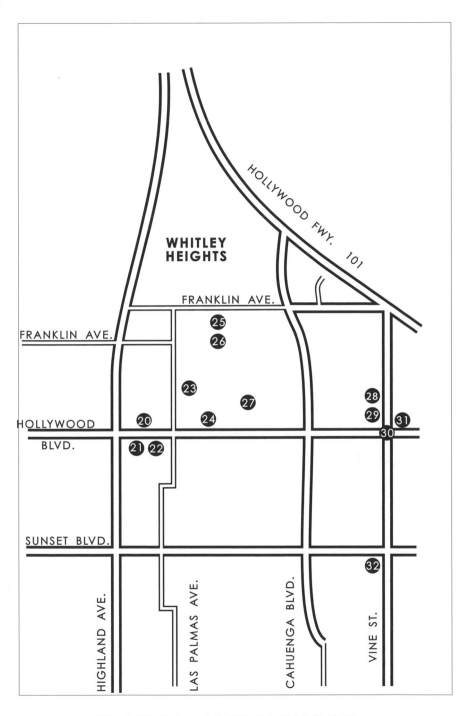

MAP 20 HOLLYWOOD

3. HIGH TOWER (at the north end of Hightower Drive, west of Camrose Drive)

Fans of the 1991 suspense thriller *Dead Again* will immediately recognize this unusual-looking Italian tower. It was here—and in the studio apartment immediately to the right of it—that the climactic scene played out. The location was deliberately chosen (and even included in the original script) because the producers wanted to show that Emma Thompson, who lived in the apartment adjacent to High Tower, was literally cut off from outside help.

The five-story tower houses an elevator which services the houses and apartments built into the hillside. The elevator is inaccessible to the public, but the area offers some interesting photo possibilities.

4. FIRST UNITED METHODIST CHURCH OF HOLLYWOOD, 6817 Franklin Avenue

This is the church where Earthlings sought refuge from invading Martians in the 1953 classic *War of the Worlds* starring Gene Barry and Ann Robinson.

The "Enchantment Under the Sea" dance in the first two *Back to the Future* movies (1985 and 1989) was filmed here, and *Sister Act* (1992) was filmed in several rooms.

5. MAGIC CASTLE, 7001 Franklin Avenue (corner of Orange Drive)

This Victorian mansion, completed in 1908, is now an exclusive private club for magicians. You have to be a member or an invited guest to get in.

6. HIGHLAND GARDENS (formerly the Landmark Hotel), 7047 Franklin Avenue (corner of Outpost Drive)

Janis Joplin died of a heroin overdose in room 105 of this Hollywood hotel on October 4, 1970. She was 27.

Hollywood's High Tower, where the climactic scene in *Dead Again* was played out.

7. YAMASHIRO RESTAURANT, 1999 N. Sycamore Avenue, (323) 466-5125

Yamashiro means "mountain palace" and that is what the restaurant is: an exact replica of a Japanese palace located in the Yamashiro mountains near Kyoto, Japan. Standing on a hillside some 250 feet above Hollywood Boulevard, and offering a panoramic view of the city, the restaurant was originally a private estate commissioned by two brothers who sold Oriental antiques. In 1914, hundreds of skilled craftspersons were brought from Japan to duplicate the Yamashiro mansion.

The restaurant was later turned into a military school and at one point was converted into apartments where several celebrities, including Richard Pryor and Pernell Roberts, lived. In 1968 Yamashiro was transformed into a restaurant. It served as the officers' club in *Sayonara* (1957) and often doubles as Japan in commercials and television productions.

8. OZZIE AND HARRIET HOUSE, 1822 Camino Palmero

The Nelson family—Ozzie, Harriet, David and Ricky—lived here for over 25 years, and the outside of the house was used in their long-running (1952-66) ABC situation comedy, "The Adventures of Ozzie and Harriet." According to Laurie Jacobson's book *Hollywood Haunted,* subsequent owners claimed the house is haunted by a ghost who would get frisky with the owner's wife.

9. JIM HENSON COMPANY, 1416 N. La Brea Avenue (just south of Sunset)

This historic studio is now the headquarters of the multimedia company that created the Muppets. A statue of Kermit the Frog stands at the studio's entrance.

The studio itself was initially built in 1919 by Charlie Chaplin, who made his classics *Modern Times, City Lights,* and *The Great Dictator* here. Between 1966 and 1999 it was the headquarters of A & M Records, which recorded artists such as Sting, Janet Jackson, Sheryl Crow, Amy Grant, Bryan Adams, and Rita Coolidge. It was here—in the late 1970s—that the late Beatle George Harrison met his second wife, Olivia Arias, and rescued her from a career as an A&M secretary. In 1985, 45 top pop stars, including Michael Jackson, Bruce Springsteen, Stevie Wonder, Tina Turner, Cyndi Lauper, Lionel Ritchie, and Diana Ross, recorded "We Are the World" in A&M Studios.

(Note: Rock fans might be interested to know that just off the map—at 7439 Sunset Boulevard—is the Sunset Grill, the eatery immortalized in The Eagles' song.)

10. KODAK THEATER, 6801 Hollywood Boulevard
The multipurpose theater, which hosts major concerts, plays, "American Idol" finales, and visiting Broadway productions, became the permanent home of the Academy Awards in 2002.

The theater now offers tours Wednesdays through Sundays between 11:00 a.m. and 2:00 p.m. For prices and information call (323) 308-6363.

The theater is surrounded by an upscale retail and entertainment complex called Hollywood & Highland. The complex includes retail stores, a six-screen expansion of Grauman's Chinese Theater, the four-star Renaissance Hollywood Hotel, restaurants, nightclubs, and a television studio.

Hollywood & Highland's three-story center court— the Babylon Courtyard—is fashioned after the largest movie set ever built: the city of Babylon in D. W. Griffith's

The Grand Arch at Hollywood & Highland.

The Kodak Theater.

1916 epic, *Intolerance*. The court includes giant pillars topped by two 33-foot-tall replicas of the set's original elephant sculptures.

Hollywood & Highland also includes a 150-foot-tall Egyptian-themed Grand Arch, which is slanted so that the Hollywood sign is perfectly framed within this portal. Public artwork within the complex includes a serpentine mosaic path, The Road to Hollywood, which has black marble panels containing stories of how people came to Hollywood and broke into the business. The path leads to what press reports describe as a fiberglass daybed—or as Hollywood cognoscenti call it, "the casting couch."

MOVIES FILMED AT
HOLLYWOOD & HIGHLAND

- *THE ITALIAN JOB* (2003): Sean Green engineered a massive traffic jam to foil Ed Norton's gateway. All vehicular traffic was stopped for six days to film the scene.

- *HOLLYWOOD HOMICIDE* (2003): Josh Harnett pursued a villain throughout the complex.

- *STUCK ON YOU* (2003): In the complex's Highlands nightclub, Matt Damon and Greg Kinnear battled bullies who mocked them as conjoined twins.

- *COLLATERAL* (2004): Tom Cruise, playing a hired hitman, killed a businessman in the Renaissance Hotel's presidential suite while his daughters watched television downstairs. A large photograph of the downtown L.A. skyline fooled viewers into believing the scene was filmed there.

11. GRAUMAN'S CHINESE THEATER, 6925

Hollywood Boulevard, (323) 464-8111

The Chinese Theater, which is undoubtedly the most famous theater in the world, opened in 1927 with the premiere of Cecil B. DeMille's *King of Kings*. Its forecourt includes the hand and footprints of about 200 Hollywood legends—although some have left other trademarks, including Jimmy Durante's nose, Harpo Marx's harp, Sonja Henje's ice skates, Betty Grable's legs, Al Jolson's knee, and Donald Duck's webbed feet.

The theater still holds inscription ceremonies. Honorees include Warren Beatty, Nicolas Cage, Jim Carrey, Jackie Chan, Sean Connery, Kirk and Michael Douglas, Harrison Ford, Morgan Freeman, Richard Gere, Mel Gibson, Danny Glover, Whoopi Goldberg, Tom Hanks, Ron Howard, Martin Lawrence, Al Pacino, Meryl Streep, Arnold Schwarzenegger, Denzel Washington, and Bruce Willis.

In 1949 the 1,492-seat theater also hosted the Academy Awards.

A 30-minute VIP Tour is offered thrice a day. Call (323) 465-4VIP for information.

12. SITE OF BOBBY FULLER'S SUPPOSED "SUICIDE BY GASOLINE," 1776 N. Sycamore Street

Just half a block south of Janis Joplin's suicide site is the death site of another famous 1960s rock and roller: Bobby Fuller. Fuller is best remembered for his 1965 hit song "I Fought the Law" (and, of course, the law won). He seemed to have unlimited potential.

Fuller was found dead in the front seat of his car, parked in the driveway of his apartment at 1776 N. Sycamore Street. The coroner ruled that he died by "ingestion of gasoline," but whether he drank the gasoline voluntarily remains a mystery.

13. "SYDNEY BRISTOW" APARTMENT, El Cadiz Apartments, 1719 Sycamore Street

During the first two years of the ABC spy drama "Alias," this building was depicted as the residence of Sydney Bristow (Jennifer Garner), who shared an apartment with her roommate, Francie (Merrin Dungy).

14. THE HOLLYWOOD WALK OF FAME

Conceived by the Hollywood Chamber of Commerce in the late 1950s as a tribute to artists who have made significant contributions to the film, radio, television and recording industries, the Walk of Fame has become a promotional tool used by celebrities to plug their new movies, albums and concert tours.

The "honor" costs $25,000 and is usually paid for by the studio or recording company. One notable exception was Liza Minnelli. Her fan club held bake sales to pay for her star.

The walk now includes over 2,300 stars and extends from Hollywood Boulevard between LaBrea and Gower Street, and Vine Street between Sunset Boulevard and Yucca Street. The Chamber publishes a "Walk the Walk" brochure that includes the exact addresses where celebrities' stars can be located, and a 2.5 hour walking tour of the boulevard.

To obtain the brochure, send a SASE to the Hollywood Chamber of Commerce, 7018 Hollywood Blvd., Hollywood, CA 90028.

If you are in town, call the Hollywood Chamber of Commerce at (323) 469-8311 for a schedule of their forthcoming induction ceremonies. Or check a private web site, www.seeing-stars.com.

A premiere at Grauman's Chinese Theater, circa 1964.

Tom Selleck's star on the Walk of Fame.

15. HOLLYWOOD ROOSEVELT HOTEL, 7000 Hollywood Boulevard, (323) 466-7000.

The hotel's Blossom Room was the site of the first Academy Awards ceremony in 1929. That year the awards were called the Merit Awards and Janet Gaynor and Emil Jennings were honored as best actor and actress, while *Wings* took honors as best feature.

The hotel's former nightclub, the Cinegrill, offered performances from well-known singers, and, along with the Blossom Room and the hotel lobby, has been a frequent site for location filming. The strip tease show in *Beverly Hills Cop II* (1987) as well as a few of Michelle Pfeiffer's nightclub scenes in *The Fabulous Baker Boys* (1989) were filmed in the Cinegrill.

Various parts of the hotel, including the roof, were also featured in *Charlie's Angels 2: Full Throttle* (2002). It was at the Roosevelt that fallen angel Demi Moore tried to sell the identities of enrollees in the Witness Protection Program.

16. EL CAPITAN THEATER, 6838 Hollywood Boulevard (corner of Orchid), (323) 467-7674

This Art Deco movie palace, which was restored in 1991, is one of Hollywood's architectural jewels. It is also the venue for Disney world premieres and the highest grossing single screen theater in the country. ABC's "The Jimmy Kimmel Show" is filmed here.

17. THE HOLLYWOOD MUSEUM, 1660 N. Highland Avenue

Permanent collections in this museum, dedicated to preserving the history and heritage of Hollywood, include Hannibal Lecter's jail cell from *Silence of the Lambs* (1991); the spaceship, props, and costumes from the original *Planet of the Apes* (1968); costumes and wardrobes of celebrities, including Nicole Kidman's Oscar-winning costumes from *Moulin Rouge* (2001), and Tom Cruise's outfits from *Minority Report* (2002); and tributes to Marilyn Monroe and Bob Hope.

The art deco building itself is historic: it was once the headquarters of Hollywood makeup czar Max Factor's cosmetic empire. The first floor of the four-story building recreates his makeup rooms. For hours and information about lectures and guided tours, call (323) 464-7776.

18. HOLLYWOOD HIGH SCHOOL, 1521 N. Highland Avenue

Until Hollywood declined in the mid-1960s, Hollywood High—and its drama department—served as sort of an unofficial actor's training ground for the studios. The school's alumni include Jason Robards, James Garner, Carol Burnett, Stephanie Powers, Linda Evans, John Ritter, Rick and David Nelson, Mickey Rooney, Judy Garland, Lawrence Fishburne, Swoozie Kurtz, Barbara Hershey, Mike Farrell, Charlene Tilton, Denise Crosby, Scott Baio, Tim Burton, Rita Wilson, and Brandy.

In *Hollywood High: The History of America's Most Famous Public (High) School*, John Blumenthal writes that Hollywood High started going downhill in 1968 when the Los Angeles school board drastically shrank the Hollywood district boundaries: "As a result, upper-middle-class areas like Toluca Lake and Studio City, which had once sent their children to Hollywood High, were suddenly located in another district." An English teacher called that a turning point: 'In one blow, we lost the cream of our students.'" By the mid-1970s, Blumenthal writes, "most recent alumni were clerk-typists, salespeople, [or] factory workers."

19. FORMER SITE OF THE TOP HAT CAFE, 1500 N. Highland Avenue (at the northeast corner of Sunset)

It was at a malt shop once located at this site, not at Schwab's Pharmacy, that Lana Turner, then a student at Hollywood High, was "discovered" and turned into star. Turner told *Los Angeles Times* columnist Jack Smith that she cut a typing class and was in the shop when she was approached by nightclub owner and *Hollywood Reporter* publisher Billy Wilkerson, who asked her: "How would you like to be in the movies?" Turner said her response was: "I don't know—I'll have to ask my mother."

20. HOLLYWOOD WAX MUSEUM, 6767 Hollywood Boulevard, (323) 462-8860

The world's only wax museum dedicated to showcasing Hollywood stars features more than 180 intricately-crafted, lifelike figures of entertainment icons set in memorable movie and TV scenes. Among them: Keanu Reeves in *The Matrix Reloaded* (2003), Russell Crowe in *Gladiator* (2000), Angelina Jolie in *Lara Croft: Tomb Raider* (2002), and the cast of Seinfeld.

Marilyn Monroe, the Beatles, 'N Sync, Frankenstein, Freddy Krueger, and political leaders are also immortalized in wax.

21. GUINNESS WORLD RECORDS MUSEUM, 6764 Hollywood Boulevard, (323) 463-6433

Records from the great to the gross are celebrated in this museum, which covers the bests in entertainment, escapades, sports feats, space adventures, technological accomplishments, animal acts, natural phenomena, and human endeavors. The stories of these records are told through videos, touch screen challenges, talking holographs, and other 3-D displays.

22. EGYPTIAN THEATER, 6712 Hollywood Boulevard, (323) 466-FILM

Built by Sid Grauman in 1922, five years before the opening of the Chinese Theater, this was Hollywood's first movie palace. One of the more architecturally unusual buildings in Hollywood, the Egyptian is now the headquarters of American Cinematheque, a nonprofit cultural group dedicated to filmmaking heritage. Private group tours can be arranged by calling (323) 461-2020.

23. *"PRETTY WOMAN"* HOTEL, 1738 N. Las Palmas Avenue (at Yucca Street)

In *Pretty Woman* (1990), Julia Roberts lived—and was eventually rescued by Richard Gere—at the Las Palmas Hotel.

(Note: Walking around this neighborhood at night is not recommended.)

24. MUSSO & FRANK GRILL, 6667 Hollywood Boulevard, (323) 467-7788 or (323) 467-5123

Musso & Frank pride themselves on being the oldest existing restaurant in Hollywood. It is still frequented by entertainment industry types.

The restaurant was seen in the opening credits of the short-lived television show about a young Hollywood agent, "The Fabulous Teddy Z," and was where, in the 2001 remake of *Oceans 11*, George Clooney convinced Brad Pitt to join his Vegas casino caper.

In the movie *Ed Wood* (1994), director Tim Burton filmed a scene at the restaurant in which Wood, who is regarded by many as the most inept director in movie history, met one of the most famous, Orson Welles. Johnny Depp played Wood while Vincent D'Onofrio played Welles.

25. MONTECITO APARTMENTS, 6650 Franklin Avenue (at Cherokee Avenue)

Ronald Reagan rented an apartment at the Montecito when he first moved to Hollywood. He lived here between 1937 and 1939, while working as a contract player for Warner Bros.

Gene Wilder, Mickey Rooney, George C. Scott, Julie Harris, and Gene Hackman also lived in this former resident hotel, which is now an apartment building for senior citizens and handicapped people.

26. ONE-TIME "WIZARD OF OZ" HOME, 1749 Cherokee Avenue

Beloved children's author L. Frank Baum, who wrote *The Wonderful Wizard of Oz* in 1903 (later filmed as *The Wizard of Oz*) lived here in a house he dubbed "Ozcot" in the early 1910s. At the time Baum tried unsuccessfully to become a movie producer. The property is now a rundown empty lot.

27. FONTENOY TOWERS, 1811 N. Whitley Avenue (north of Hollywood Boulevard)

Parajournalist Matt Drudge lived and worked in a cramped ninth-floor apartment at the Fontenoy when he broke the story about President Bill Clinton's affair with intern Monica Lewinsky.

According to the building's manager, Johnny Depp and Nicolas Cage also once lived in the building. Drudge now lives in Florida.

28. (FORMER) KNICKERBOCKER HOTEL, 1714 N. Ivar Street

Now a retirement home, the Knickerbocker was the hotel where Marilyn Monroe and Joe DiMaggio honeymooned in 1954, and Houdini's widow conducted séances, hoping to reconnect with her departed husband.

Former hotel resident William Frawley, who played Fred Mertz on "I Love Lucy," dropped dead of a heart attack in front of the hotel on March 3, 1966.

Contrary to claims made by some tour guides, the Knickerbocker was not the "Heartbreak Hotel" that Elvis sang about. That song was released before Elvis and his entourage took over the eleventh floor penthouse while he filmed *Love Me Tender* (1956). So many groupies descended on the hotel during that summer of 1956 that The King was forced to relocate to the Regent Beverly Wilshire.

29. CAPITOL RECORDS, 1750 N. Vine Street

The Capitol Tower, which was designed in 1954, is one of Hollywood's most identifiable landmarks. It is a circular office building resembling a stack of records with a needle on top (although the architect, Welton Becket, denies that he created the look intentionally).

Capitol's artists over the years have included Frank Sinatra, the Beatles, Nat "King" Cole, Bing Crosby, the Beach Boys, Tina Turner, Donnie Osmond, the Doobie Brothers, Heart, Hammer, and the Steve Miller Band. The company's Gold Awards are on display in the lobby, but the company does not offer tours for the public.

30. CORNER OF HOLLYWOOD AND VINE

The corner of Hollywood and Vine became famous in the early 1920s, when the headquarters of several major studios (Paramount, Fox, Columbia, and Warner Bros.), NBC and other radio stations, and a Brown Derby were located there. According to Richard Adkins, an historical preservationist, the intersection became famous because "so many stars were working and spending their free time

The Capitol Records Tower, one of Hollywood's most famous
landmarks.

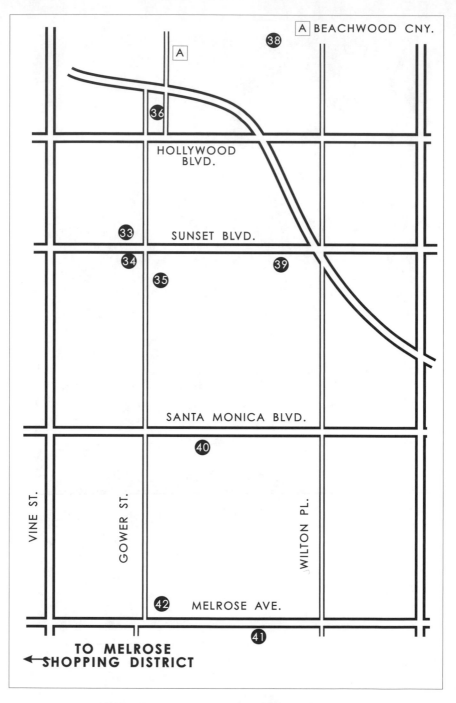

A BEACHWOOD CNY.

A

38

36

HOLLYWOOD BLVD.

SUNSET BLVD.

33

34

35

39

SANTA MONICA BLVD.

40

VINE ST.

GOWER ST.

WILTON PL.

42

MELROSE AVE.

41

TO MELROSE
← SHOPPING DISTRICT

MAP 21 HOLLYWOOD

there." However, when most of the studios moved to the suburbs, the area around Hollywood and Vine deteriorated considerably. Instead of attracting businesses, it became a magnet for runaways, hookers, and drug dealers.

With the help of local and city visionaries, the intersection is making a slow but steady comeback. Helping considerably was a resplendently restored Pantages Theater, located just a few steps from the corner; and several nearby nightclubs which attracted young partying celebrities.

If you visit the area, be sure to look at the northwest and northeast sidewalks, where you will find Walk of Fame stars saluting Apollo XI astronauts Neil Armstrong, Edward Aldrin, and Michael Collins. In true Hollywood fashion, the astronauts were honored not for being the first men to journey to the moon, but because they appeared in an "outstanding television production"!

31. PANTAGES THEATER, 6233 Hollywood Boulevard (just east of Vine)

Another extraordinary example of Art Deco architecture, the Pantages was the site of the Academy Awards in the 1950s. It now a venue for major theatrical productions.

32. CINERAMA DOME, 6360 Sunset Boulevard (corner of Ivar Avenue, one block west of Vine Street)

The Cinerama movie craze—in which movies were presented on three screens to give the moviegoer the illusion of being engaged in the action—died in the 1960s, but this geodesic-domed theater, built exclusively for those films, lives on as a conventional movie theater which is now part of a multiplex. The theater is now called the Arclight Dome.

33. COLUMBIA SQUARE, 6121 Sunset Boulevard (between El Centro Avenue and Gower Street)

The first motion picture studio in Hollywood—the Nestor Film Company—was originally located on this site.

Nestor later merged with Universal Studios. In 1938 CBS built Columbia Square Complex, which formerly housed Los Angeles' channel 2 and still houses the CBS-owned radio station KNX.

34. GOWER GULCH, 6098 Sunset Boulevard (at Gower Street)

During the late teens and early 1920s, a number of independent studios—many of them fly-by-nights— operated in this stretch of Sunset Boulevard, and extras looking for work used to hang out in this area. Many came dressed in costume as cowboys and Indians, and someone named the area "Gower Gulch." To pay homage to that era the developers of the shopping center designed it to resemble a Western street.

35. SUNSET GOWER STUDIOS, 1438 N. Gower Street (at Sunset Boulevard)

Once the home of Columbia Studios, Sunset Gower is now a privately owned rental studio used for television, motion picture, and commercial filming. *The Good German* (2006) and TV's "Heroes," "The Golden Girls," and "The Fresh Prince of Bel-Air" filmed here. When you drive by, you will see billboards with the names of the shows currently taping on the lot.

36. BEACHWOOD CANYON, at the intersection of Franklin and Beachwood drives

As you drive north on Beachwood Drive, you will see both traditional and unusual architecture, particularly the turreted apartments on the corner of Scenic Drive. You will also find sites of entertainment interest. The first is Monroe Manor, an apartment at 2232 Beachwood Drive. This building was depicted as Matt LeBlanc's apartment in the short-lived (2004-2006) "Friends" spinoff, "Joey." Ironically, LeBlanc had lived there himself (in Apartment 16) in his early Hollywood days.

A few blocks down, at 2428 Beachwood Drive, is the home of Peg Entwhistle, a successful Broadway actress who was unable to make the transition to Hollywood. Believing she was washed up at the age of 24, Entwhistle ended it all by jumping off the famous Hollywood Sign. Her first acting offer came in the mail the following day.

Continue driving north on Beachwood and approximately one mile north of Franklin you will pass, just south of the intersection of Beachwood and Westshire drives, the stone gates to Hollywoodland, one of the first housing developments in Southern California. You will be able to see the offices of Hollywoodland Realty when you reach Beachwood and Westshire. This is the real estate company that first sold homes in the Hollywood Hills and tbat erected the Hollywood sign—which originally advertised "Hollywoodland." The last four letters, of course, were later removed by the Hollywood Chamber of Commerce after they fell into disrepair.

The western part of Westshire is where the pod people chased Kevin McCarthy and Dana Wynter in the 1955 classic *Invasion of the Body Snatchers* (subsequently remade three times).

If you continue north on Beachwood and follow Ledgewood Drive west, you will proceed up a narrow, windy road and make a hard right on Deronda Drive. Across from 3374 Deronda Drive is an open space where you can take pictures of the Hollywood Sign up close.

37. CELEBRITY CENTRE INTERNATIONAL, CHURCH OF SCIENTOLOGY (WEST COAST HEADQUARTERS), 5930 Franklin Avenue

Scientology is a religion that claims 10 million members worldwide. *Time* magazine once attacked it as a cult and "a ruthless global scam." The religion de-emphasizes God, believes that Americans should throw away their antidepressants and other drugs, psychiatry is nuts, and that we all descended from aliens from outer space.

Hollywood certainly has plenty of adherents, including Tom Cruise, John Travolta and Kelly Preston, Kirstie Alley, two stars from NBC's "My Name is Earl" (Jason Lee and Ethan Suplee), Jenna Elfman ("Dharma and Greg"), Leah Remini ("The King of Queens"), and Jennifer Lewis.

Scientology owns quite a bit of property in Hollywood, including this seven-story Normandy castle, the Chateau Elysee, which, in the 1930s and 1940s, was the home of numerous Hollywood stars. The church's restaurant is open to the public.

38. KTLA, 5858 Sunset Boulevard (between Bronson and Van Ness)

This neo-colonial mansion was the original home of Warner Bros. and the site of the 1927 filming of *The Jazz Singer*, the first feature film which featured synchronized dialogue. When Warner moved its main headquarters to Burbank in 1929, this facility was used to produce "Bugs Bunny," "Porky Pig," and other Warner animated cartoons. Today the building houses the independent television station KTLA (Los Angeles' channel 5). KTLA does not offer a tour.

39. HOLLYWOOD FOREVER CEMETERY, 6000 Santa Monica Boulevard (between Gower and Van Ness Avenues)

Many of Hollywood's early greats (Rudolph Valentino, Cecil B. DeMille, Tyrone Power, and Douglas Fairbanks, Sr.) are buried here. So are Peter Finch, Peter Lorre, Carl "Alfalfa" Switzer, director John Huston, and Harry Cohn, the much-despised former president of Columbia Pictures. Legend has it that the reason Cohn's funeral was so well-attended was that many of those present wanted to make sure that he was dead.

The legendary Jayne Mansfield has a cenotaph here, but is buried in Pennsylvania. Mansfield was 33 when died in a car crash. Her children, including "Law & Order: SVU" actress Mariska Hargitay, were not injured in the crash.

For years a mysterious veiled "Lady in Black" brought flowers to Rudolph Valentino's tomb on the anniversary of Valentino's death. Cemetery curators still occasionally find lipstick on his crypt.

The Jewish section of the cemetery features the graves of mobster Bugsy Siegel as well as Mel Blanc, "The Man of 1,000 Voices," including Bugs Bunny and Porky Pig. Blanc's epitaph is a take-off of Porky Pig's cartoon salutation: "That's all, folks."

Visiting hours are 8:00 A.M. to 5:00 P.M. throughout the grounds. Maps of the stars' graves are available for sale at the main entrance for those wishing to tour the site.

The cemetery also offers 90-minute tours at noon on the first Saturday of every month. No reservations are required. For prices and additional information e-mail tours@forevernetwork.com.

Mel Blanc's gravestone at Hollywood Forever Cemetery.

The Paramount Studios gate.

40. RALEIGH STUDIOS, 650 N. Bronson Avenue (on both the southeast and southwest corners of Melrose)

Raleigh may or may not be the oldest continually operating studio in Hollywood (KCET makes the same claim, and the dispute is probably over the word "continually"). In any event, Raleigh is a rental studio used primarily for commercials, although some television shows, feature films, and music videos have also been filmed here. When the studio was called the Producers' Studio in the 1960s, Ronald Reagan hosted "Death Valley Days" here.

Episodes from "The Life of Riley," "Gunsmoke," "The Adventures of Superman," and "Perry Mason," were also filmed on the lot. Not open to the public.

41. PARAMOUNT STUDIOS, 5555 Melrose Avenue

Paramount is the only major studio still located in Hollywood. One of its main attractions is its famous wrought-iron side gate, at the corner of Bronson Avenue and Marathon Street—which is not to be confused with the main gate on Melrose. The side gate was immortalized in *Sunset Boulevard* (1950) and has appeared in countless other movies.

For tickets to TV tapings and tour information, call Paramount Guest Relations at (323) 956-4848. Paramount offers a two-hour backlot tour four times a day.

(Note: After driving past Paramount you have a number of options for additional touring. You can make a left turn onto Rossmore Avenue and do the Hancock Park/Wilshire District tour—or you can continue west on Melrose for about a mile and a half until you reach La Brea. Between La Brea and Fairfax is the world-famous Melrose Avenue shopping district. Melrose is a popular hangout among yuppies and punk rockers.

The nighttime soap opera "Melrose Place," which aired on Fox between 1992 and 1999, sometimes filmed on Melrose Avenue; but do not go looking for the apartment building there. For exterior shots, the producers used an apartment building in Los Feliz (see page 192). The interior courtyard, including the pool area, and the interiors of the apartments, existed only on a studio backlot in the city of Santa Clarita, some thirty miles north of Los Angeles.

Perched atop a small hill which overlooks the Hollywood Freeway, Castle Ivar (2061 Ivar Avenue) seems ready to withstand an army of armor clad invaders.

DID YOU KNOW THAT...

- Two infamous assassins spent time in Hollywood? James Earl Ray, in the months prior to the slaying of Martin Luther King, Jr., lived at 1535 Serrano Avenue. John Hinckley lived at 1125 El Centro Street, five years before he shot and wounded Ronald Reagan and several others.

- C. C. Brown, the now-defunct ice cream parlor on the 7100 block of Hollywood Boulevard, fudged its claim that it invented the ice cream sundae?

- A number of celebrities live in the fashionable hills north of Hollywood Boulevard? Bob Barker, Rebecca DeMornay, Will Ferrell, Brian Greene, Felicity Huffman and William H. Macy, Penny Marshall, Ben Stiller, and Charlize Theron own homes in the prestigious Outpost Estates, by Outpost Drive. Ben Affleck lived just off Outpost but sold his home to his friend, director Kevin Smith. Patrick Stewart, who played Jean-Luc Picard on "Star Trek: The Next Generation," apparently lived next door to Affleck. Affleck told a reporter that Stewart once bumped into his former girlfriend Gwyneth Paltrow, and asked: "Do you stay at . . . " and gave Affleck's address. "And she said, 'Uh . . . yeah.' And he gave her this look and said, 'well, you should really get some blinds.'"

- Debra Messing, star of the NBC comedy "Will and Grace," lived at 2000 N. Curson Drive before buying Renee Zellweger's Bel Air home in 2004?

- Matthew Perry, who starred on the NBC sitcom "Friends," lived at 7204 Chelan Way between 1995 and 2001?

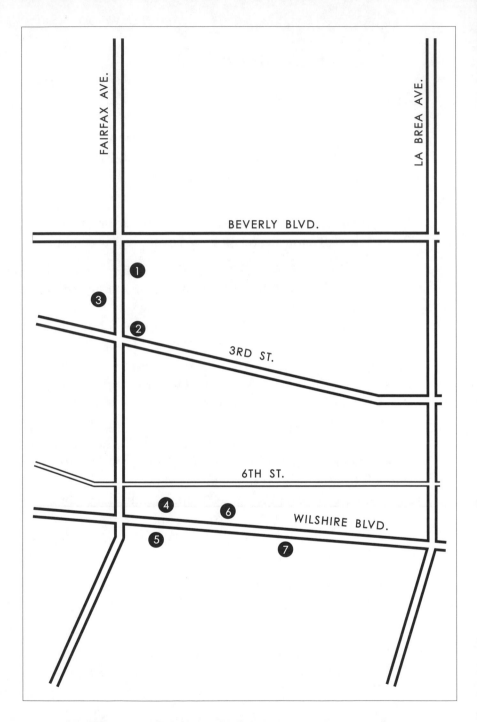

MAP 22   FAIRFAX AND THE MIRACLE MILE

FAIRFAX AND
THE MIRACLE MILE

1. CBS TELEVISION CITY, 7800 Beverly Boulevard (at Fairfax Avenue)

CBS does not offer a tour of its facility, but tickets for "The Price is Right" are available at their walk-in booth on Fairfax, or by writing to CBS at 7800 Beverly Boulevard, Los Angeles, CA 90036.

2. FARMER'S MARKET, 3rd Street and Fairfax Avenue

The *Los Angeles Times* placed Farmer's Market at the top of its list of the ten best places to spot celebrities in L.A. The *Times* reported that: "A wide spectrum of celebs is known to meander through the stalls . . . The soap opera stars from CBS are there to grab lunch."

3. FARMER'S DAUGHTER HOTEL, 115 S. Fairfax Avenue

The hotel has been called "The Price is Right" Motel because so many contestants stay there. Academy Award winner Charlize Theron and her mother lived here when she first moved to Hollywood.

4. LOS ANGELES COUNTY MUSEUM OF ART, 5905 Wilshire Boulevard

The museum has appeared in several movies, including *L.A. Story* (1991), in which Steve Martin, a real-life avid art collector, was the only one in a foursome to see a naked woman in a work of abstract art. In *The Player* (1992), Cher and dozens of other celebrities, playing themselves, attended a gala studio event.

Featuring some of the country's best art, the museum is worth a visit. For hours and additional information, call (323) 857-6000.

5. MUTUAL BENEFIT LIFE BUILDING, 5900 Wilshire Boulevard

In 1989's *Miracle Mile*, a pre-"E.R." Anthony Edwards learned that L.A. was the target of a nuclear strike and desperately tried to arrange helicopter get-away from the roof of this 31-story-tall building. Edwards and his girlfriend, played by Ware Winningham, got as far as the La Brea Tar Pits across the street.

6. LA BREA TAR PITS AND THE GEORGE C. PAGE MUSEUM OF LA BREA DISCOVERIES, 5801 Wilshire Boulevard, (323) 857-6301

The Pits are pools of asphaltum and crude oil that have trapped more than 200 varieties of birds, mammals, plants, reptiles and insects, some dating back to prehistoric times. While the Pits were ground zero for the eruption in *Volcano* (1997), scientists assure us that the only real-life dangers lurking beneath the Pits are L.A.'s crazy quilt of earthquake faults.

7. WILSHIRE COURTYARD, 5750 and 5760 Wilshire Boulevard

Twin office buildings which house (in addition to banks and attorneys' offices) *Daily Variety*, *Us* magazine, E! Entertainment, and several production companies, including one founded by the late Aaron Spelling. Spelling, the producer of "Melrose Place," used the courtyard for the exterior shots of D & D Advertising.

HANCOCK PARK AND THE WILSHIRE DISTRICT

1. "HAPPY DAYS" HOME, 565 N. Cahuenga Avenue (south of Melrose Avenue)

Served as the Cunningham home in the long-running (1974-84) ABC sitcom "Happy Days."

2. FORMER FRAN DRESCHER HOME, 530 N. Lillian Way

Fran Drescher lived here, one block west of the El Royale, in the 1990s when she starred in the CBS sitcom "The Nanny."

3. FORMER HOME OF MAE WEST, 570 N. Rossmore Avenue

For 48 years (from 1932 until her death in 1980), Mae West lived in the penthouse of the Ravenswood Apartments.

4. EL ROYALE APARTMENTS, 450 N. Rossmore Avenue (at Rosewood Avenue)

For years a story circulated that John F. Kennedy stayed here during the 1960 Democratic National Convention in Los Angeles, even though his official campaign headquarters was at the Biltmore Hotel downtown. Sandra Griffin, the El Royale's property manager, checked into the stories, and reported that JFK did not stay at the El Royale, but stayed in room 301 at an apartment building (formerly a hotel, the Rossmore House) two doors down the street—at 522 N. Rossmore Avenue. The book *Johnny, We Hardly Knew Ye* by former JFK aides Kenneth P. O'Donnell and David F. Powers with Joe McCarthy, confirms this, saying that Powers found the hideaway apartment so JFK could "sleep and eat a quiet breakfast, away from the turmoil at the Biltmore."

Tour buses which drive past the El Royale can continue to note it as a point of interest, though. Several celebrities have lived there at one time or another, including Ben Stiller; Cameron Diaz; Harry Cohn, the former president of Columbia Pictures; William Frawley, who played Fred on "I Love Lucy;" George Raft; Loretta Young; Nicolas Cage; and Clark Gable, who lived here with his second wife, Ria, in 1933. One columnist now calls it "sort of a dormitory for Hollywood agents."

The lobby of the building was seen in *Switch* (1991) starring Ellen Barkin and in *Other People's Money* (1991), where it served as Penelope Anne Miller's apartment.

5. FORMER NAT KING COLE HOME, 401 Muirfield Road

Cole bought this English Tudor mansion in 1948 as a wedding present for his bride, Maria, shocking and angering his WASPy neighbors, who were not used to having blacks around. According to *Lamparski's Hidden Hollywood* by Richard Lamparski: "Larchmont residents called a property owners' meeting shortly after the Coles moved in. An attorney for the group summed up its feelings when he said that many of those present were born and raised in Larchmont: 'We are greatly disturbed at the prospect of having undesirables living here.' Cole responded: 'I'm relieved to hear how concerned you all are about your neighborhood. I feel exactly the same way. I'd like you all to

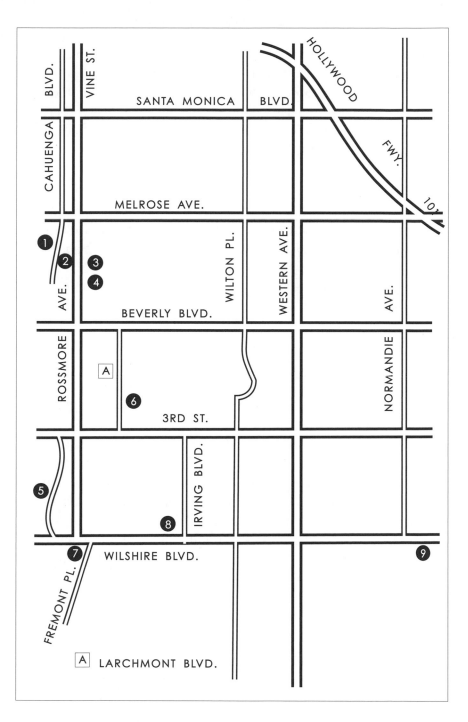

MAP 23 HANCOCK PARK & WILSHIRE DISTRICT

know that if my wife or I see anyone undesirable in Larchmont we'll be the first to object. Thank you.'"

Other notables who lived on Muirfield include Howard Hughes, whose first Los Angeles home was at 211; Buster Keaton, who owned a home at 543; and Dan Blocker who lived at 555 Muirfield Road.

6. MRX PHARMACY, 150 N. Larchmont Boulevard

During the first two seasons of "MacGyver"—when the show was filmed in Los Angeles in 1985 and 1986— Richard Dean Anderson (MacGyver) lived in the loft above the pharmacy.

Many of the chase scenes from the Keystone Cop comedies were also filmed on Larchmont.

7. 119 FREMONT PLACE, between 4400 and 4500 Wilshire Boulevard

This was Michael Douglas and Kathleen Turner's home in *War of the Roses* (1989). The house is in a gated community and is not visible from the street.

Fremont Place has always attracted celebrities. Muhammed Ali lived for years at 55 Fremont Place; Mary Pickford and her mother lived across the street at 56; and Cliff Robertson lived at 97 Fremont Place when the David Begelman scandal broke. Mick Jagger also lived on Fremont Place in the mid-1980s. Sylvester Stallone's house in *Rocky,* according to location manager Mike Alvarado, was also on this street.

8. SITE OF THE "SUNSET BOULEVARD" MANSION (located at the northwest corner of Wilshire and Irving Boulevards, at what is now 4155 Wilshire Boulveard)

An office building is located here now, but in 1950 Gloria Swanson's mansion in the classic *Sunset Boulevard,* stood here. The mansion once belonged to billionaire J. Paul Getty and was also featured in *Rebel Without a Cause* (1955).

9. SITE OF THE AMBASSADOR HOTEL, 3400 Wilshire Boulevard

The Ambassador was once a Hollywood hot spot and is perhaps best known as the site where Robert F. Kennedy was assassinated while running for the presidency in 1968. The hotel closed in 1990 and for the next 15 years was used as a location site until it was bought and torn down by the L.A. Unified School District.

In addition to playing itself in Tom Hanks' directorial debut, *That Thing You Do!*, the Ambassador was the nightclub in *The Mask*, *The Aviator,* the Nashville bar where Robin Wright stripped in *Forrest Gump*, the site of *Romy and Michele's High School Reunion*, Gary Sinise and Kevin Bacon's apartments in *Apollo 13*, L'Idiot Restaurant in *L.A. Story*, the Brown Derby restaurant in *Ed Wood*, Meryl Streep's hotel in *Defending Your Life*, and both a Catskill resort and a glitzy Las Vegas showroom in Billy Crystal's *Mr. Saturday Night*.

The Academy Awards were presented in the hotel's famous Cocoanut Grove six times between 1930 and 1943. In 1947 Marilyn Monroe started as a model at the Emmaline Snively's Blue Book Modeling Agency, located at the hotel. The property is closed to the public.

JUST OFF THE MAP are a few sites which certainly are not must-sees for tourists who are in Los Angeles for just a short time, but which are worth pointing out if you happen to be driving east on Wilshire Boulevard on your way toward downtown. The first, at 757 New Hampshire Avenue, just south of Wilshire, is the apartment building depicted as Jerry Seinfeld's apartment in the hit sitcom "Seinfeld."

That building is only a few blocks from the Bryson Apartment Hotel, located at 2701 Wilshire Boulevard, at the corner of Lafayette Park Place. The Bryson was featured in Raymond Chandler's novel *The Lady in the Lake* and was where John Cusack lived in *The Grifters* (1990) and the ironic unsuccessful suicide/successful homicide was filmed in *Magnolia* (2000).

Just east of that is MacArthur Park, which borders 6th and 7th Streets on the north, and Park View on the east and Alvarado Street on the west. Richard Harris immortalized the park in his hit song "MacArthur Park." The area is not one a tourist would go to; it is one of the more dangerous areas in town.

Overlooking MacArthur Park, at 607 S. Park View Street (at the corner of Sixth Street), is the Park Plaza Hotel, which is frequently used as a film location. Ricardo Montalban's office in *The Naked Gun*, the party scene in *Less Than Zero,* James Spader's lecture in *Stargate*, the site of the Richard Nixon-Mao Tse Tung meeting in *Nixon*, and Whitney Houston's arrival at the Academy Award ceremonies in *The Bodyguard* were all filmed in or outside the hotel.

CELEBRITIES WHO LIVE IN HANCOCK PARK: Jason Alexander, Antonio Banderas and Melanie Griffith, Angela Bassett, Kathy Bates, Mr. Blackwell, Sean Hayes, Patricia Heaton, Sharon Lawrence, William Petersen, David Schwimmer, and Tony Shaloub.

Ellen DeGeneres and Anne Heche also owned two houses in Hancock Park in the late 1990s, the second at 201 S. Windsor Boulevard.

Singer Josh Groban also grew up in Hancock Park.

MULHOLLAND DRIVE AND THE HOLLYWOOD HILLS

A visit to Los Angeles would not be complete without a drive on Mulholland Drive—a windy mountain road which offers breathtaking views of the city and the San Fernando Valley, particularly at night.

Because it is so curvy, Mulholland demands your constant attention. If you make one little mistake, you can drive your car off a cliff—just like they do in the movies

Since Mulholland does demand your attention, sightseeing by car is not recommended—if you are alone. Of course, if someone else is driving, keep your eyes posted for the following landmarks.

This tour starts by Beverly Glen Boulevard (north of Beverly Hills and Bel-Air) and continues eastward until Mulholland ends by Cahuenga Boulevard—which is north of Hollywood and just west of the Hollywood Freeway.

1. MULHOLLAND ESTATES, 14111 Mulholland Drive (north side of street, between Beverly Glen Boulevard and Benedict Canyon Drive)

Exclusive gated community where Christina Aguilera, Loni Anderson, Tom Arnold, Fred Dryer, John Fogerty, Tom Jones, Shaquille O'Neal, Vanna White, and Brian Wilson either own or have owned homes.

(Eagles star Don Henley used to live in a house across the street. His home is not, however, visible from the street.)

179

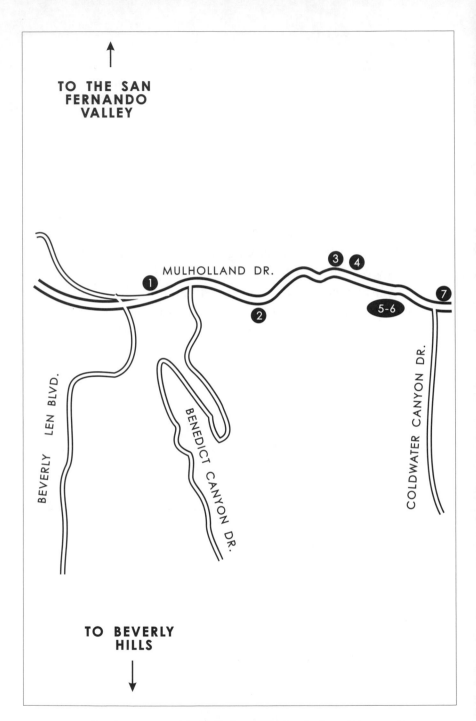

TO THE SAN
FERNANDO
VALLEY

MULHOLLAND DR.

3 4

1

2

5-6

7

BEVERLY LEN BLVD.

BENEDICT CANYON DR.

COLDWATER CANYON DR.

TO BEVERLY
HILLS

MAP 24   HOLLYWOOD HILLS

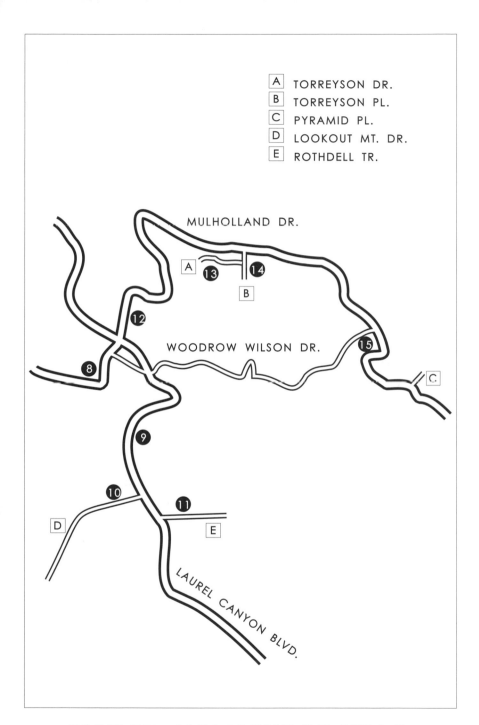

MAP 25 HOLLYWOOD HILLS

2. BEVERLY PARK (north entrance by 13100 Mulholland Drive)

This is the most exclusive of the private communities in Los Angeles; it is where Eddie Murphy, Barry Bonds, Faith Hill and Tim McGraw, L. Samuel Jackson, Magic Johnson, Martin Lawrence, Reba McIntyre, Denzel Washington, Sylvester Stallone, Rod Stewart, and Alan Thicke have homes.

Prices start at $15 million. Kelsey Grammer recently sold his house for about $25 million.

3. HOME OF WARREN BEATTY AND ANNETTE BENING, 13671 Mulholland Drive

This is not visible from the street.

4. ONE-TIME HOME OF BRUCE WILLIS AND DEMI MOORE, 13511 Mulholland Drive

This is also not visible from the street.

5. JACK NICHOLSON'S LONGTIME HOME, 12850 Mulholland Drive

This is where, in Nicholson's absence, director Roman Polanski seduced a 13-year-old model, leading to a 1977 charge of unlawful sexual intercourse to which Polanski pleaded guilty. Polanski spent 42 days undergoing psychiatric observation at Chino State Prison; and then, to avoid further jail time, fled to Europe. He now lives in permanent exile in Paris, where he continues to make films.

People magazine once wrote that in the mid-1970s Nicholson's home "became an epicenter of the era's drug-soaked social scene."

Denzel Washington's home in Beverly Park.

Eddie Murphy's home in Beverly Park.

6. MARLON BRANDO/JACK NICHOLSON COM-POUND, 12900 Mulholland Drive

Next door Brando had even worse trouble in his twelve-room compound, which is located behind the same security gate. On May 16, 1990, Brando's son Christian shot and killed Dag Drollet, the lover of Brando's daughter Cheyenne. Christian later pled guilty to a charge of voluntary manslaughter and received a ten-year prison sentence.

Marlon Brando died in 2004, and a year later Nicholson purchased the house for $5 million.

Neither house is visible from the street.

7. THE SUMMIT, 12000 Mulholland Drive

Another gated community, although not as posh as Beverly Park. Britney Spears, Gwen Stefani, Ed McMahon, Anita Pointer, Eddie Van Halen and Valerie Bertenelli, and Damon Wayans have homes here.

Jennifer Lopez married Marc Anthony in her former home here. In 2006, her house was sold for over $15 million to "No Doubt's" Gwen Stefani and her husband, Gavin Rossdale, the former frontman for the rock group Bush.

8. FORMER HOME OF RICK JAMES, 8115 Mulholland Terrace (just south of Mulholland Drive and west of Laurel Canyon Boulevard)

In 1991 the late Grammy Award-winning singer Rick James, best known for his song "Super Freak," and the mother of his son, Tanya Anne Hijazi, were charged with imprisoning and torturing a 24-year-old woman at this house. Police charged that James met the woman at a party, offered to put her up at his house, and then threatened to kill her if she left. James allegedly tied her up, forced the victim

Jack Nicholson lived in this modest bungalow for 30 years before he purchased friend and neighbor's Marlon Brando mansion next door.

One-time carpenter Harrison Ford helped build 7101 Woodrow Wilson Drive, where he lived while making Star Wars. Across the street is an imposing golden mansion that looks like a cross between a Mayan whorehouse and a Klingon dungeon.

to orally copulate Hijazi, and burned her with a crack cocaine pipe.

James, a recovering cocaine addict, beat that rap but was convicted in 1993 of a separate charge of assaulting and imprisoning another woman in another incident at the Sunset Tower Hotel on the Sunset Strip. James spent three years at the Folsom State Prison for that incident.

9. SO-CALLED "HOUDINI ESTATE," 2398 Laurel Canyon Boulevard

Just off the map, about 7/10 of a mile south of Mulholland Drive, are the ruins of an estate that several books on Hollywood identify as once belonging to Harry Houdini. About all that is left of the estate are the servants' quarters, steps which led to an Italian villa once standing on the site, and the remains of a bridge that once connected the villa with the houses located across the street on Laurel Canyon Boulevard.

Since Houdini once vowed to return from the dead, psychics still hold seances on the property, and legends persist that two ghosts—Houdini's plus the ghost of a mysterious woman dressed in green lingerie—haunt the estate.

Houdini worked on several silent films in Hollywood in 1919, but a leading Houdini expert, Manny Weltman, insists that Houdini never leased or owned the property, and that during his Hollywood stay he either stayed at a fellow magician's home or in a studio bungalow. Unfortunately, title searches of the property do not reveal who owned the estate before 1922. To protect itself against charges of false advertising, a real estate company that tried to sell the property recently advertised it as the "estate known as Harry Houdini's."

10. FORMER JONI MITCHELL, 8217 Lookout Mountain Road

Joni Mitchell lived here during the late 1960s and 1970s, when Laurel Canyon was the neighborhood of preferences for up-and-coming musicians like the Byrds, the Yardbirds, and the Doors, not to mention the Mamas and the Papas.

Mitchell's former home is the very, very fine house that her one-time live-in lover Graham Nash immortalized in the song "Our House." Crosby, Stills & Nash was born at that house after Nash joined Crosby and Stills in a 1968 jam session.

11. ONE-TIME JIM MORRISON HOME, 8217 Rothdell Trail

A mile south of Mitchell's home, right behind the Canyon Country Store, is the house that the Doors' Jim Morrison shared with his lover, Pam Courson, when the Doors rocketed to fame in the mid-1960s.

12. FORMER HOME OF "JEOPARDY!" HOST ALEX TREBEK, 7966 Mulholland Drive

13. THE CHEMOSPHERE, 7776 Torreyson Drive (one block north of Mulholland Drive)

Brian DePalma used it in his 1984 film *Body Double* as the house where down-on-his-luck actor Craig Wasson became a pawn in a bizarre murder. In the 2000 feature film *Charlie's Angels,* Drew Barrymore was shot at and crashed through the house's windows (although in that movie, because of space requirements, the house was duplicated on a stage at a cost of $180,000).

To get to the house, the occupants have to either climb more than 100 steps or take a cable car from the garage, which is on the street level, to the house's front door. The house was designed by the famed architect John Lautner, who also designed the house in *Diamonds are Forever* (1970) that James Bond rescued Willard Whyte from, after disposing of his bathing suit-clad bodyguards, Bambi and Thumper. Lautner also designed a house down the street at 7436 Mulholland that Mel Gibson brought down from its pedestal in *Lethal Weapon 2* (1989).

The best views of the Chemosphere are from the corner of Torreyson Drive and Flynn Ranch Road or from across the street at 7777 Torreyson Drive.

(Neighborhood footnote: At the time she became famous for her role in 1992's *Basic Instinct*, Sharon Stone lived across at the street at 7809 Torreyson Drive. She now lives in Beverly Hills.)

14. ERROL FLYNN'S "MULHOLLAND HOUSE,"
3100 Torreyson Place

Flynn threw wild parties here and installed one-way mirrors so he and his friends could watch his houseguests making love. After his death, the house was later owned by Richard Dreyfuss, as well as Rick Nelson, who was the last person to live in the house before it was torn down. The property—sans house—was later sold to the president of New York Seltzer for $4 million. The site was later sold to Helen Hunt, who built a 12,000 square foot home on the site. Hunt subsequently sold the property without ever moving in.

"The Flying Saucer" house featured in *Body Double* and the first *Charlie's Angels* movie.

15. "LETHAL WEAPON 2" FILMING SITE, 7436 Mulholland Drive

In the movie *Lethal Weapon 2* (1989), Mel Gibson tied the pedestal of this house to a pickup truck, and brought the house down by driving away.

Of course, the house was not really destroyed. The producers built two exact duplicates of the house—one on Stage 1 at Burbank Studios; the other in Newhall, 20 miles north of Los Angeles, and destroyed those instead.

It was the house in Newhall which plummeted to the bottom of the hill. In the movie the house was the residence of the evil ambassador of South Africa.

16. ONE-TIME MAMA CASS/RINGO STARR/DAN AYKROYD HAUNTED HOUSE, 7708 Woodrow Wilson Drive

A gated (but unfortunately not visible from the street) home at 7708 Woodrow Wilson Drive has a particularly unusual history. In the 1960s then-owner Cass Elliott of "The Mamas and the Papas" held legendary skinny-dipping parties there. In the 1970s, the home was owned by former Beatle Ringo Starr, who reportedly continued the party-hard tradition. And then, in the 1980s and 1990s it was owned by actor Dan Aykroyd, who claimed the house is haunted.

The ex-Ghostbuster told *Playboy* that piano-playing and other noises spooked some of his friends and one of his maids, and that he later discovered that someone died of a drug overdose in the living room.

Aykroyd insisted that he no problem sharing living quarters with the poltergeist. However, he did move to New York in 1997 to star in the short-lived sitcom "Soul Man," and decided to live there permanently.

HOLLYWOODLAND
AND LOS FELIZ

1. CASTILLO DEL LAGO, 6342 Mulholland Highway (corner of Canyon Lake Drive)

Madonna lived in this nine-story-tall, 32-room, Spanish-style colonial mansion; purchasing it in 1993 for $5 million and selling it three years later for roughly the same price. While living there she horrified neighbors by painting it deep red with alternating red and yellow horizontal stripes over the compound's retaining wall and bell tower. The odd color scheme only added to the home's colorful history. In past years it had reportedly been used as a bordello and gambling den.

According to Charles Lockwood's *The Guide to Hollywood and Beverly Hills*, the castle was used by mobster Bugsy Siegel in the 1930s and "fit Bugsy's security needs perfectly—or so he thought. The only entrance was through a courtyard near the bottom of the house at the end of a long, narrow, winding driveway. The police would never attack the house from this approach. Because of the house's unobstructed views, Bugsy's strong-armed men thought that they could see the police coming from all other directions. But they were wrong. One night the police stormed Castillo del Lago from a neighboring house, and Bugsy's gambling-den days were over.

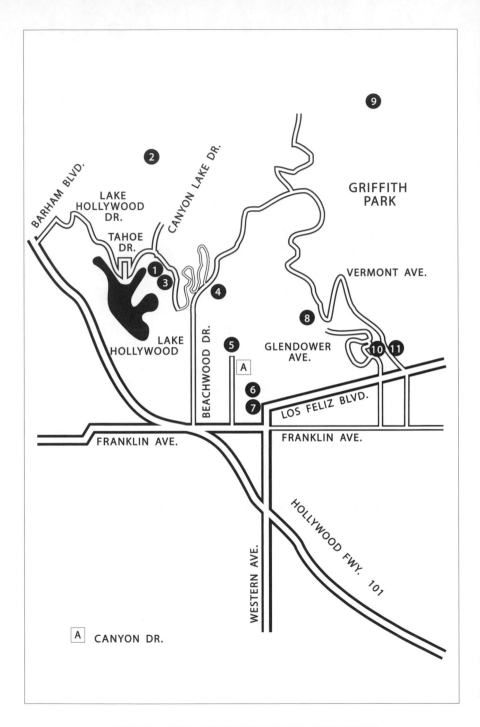

MAP 26   HOLLYWOODLAND & LOS FELIZ

The best place to view the castle is from the hiking trail which runs along its side. (Incidentally, it is possible to hike from this castle to Wolf's Lair, a historic chateau described on page 197. The trail, which is about half a mile long, provides the best views of Lake Hollywood, which was featured in both *Chinatown* (1974) and *Earthquake* (1974). In *Earthquake,* the reservoir's dam collapsed, and the ensuing flood swept away all the people and buildings in its path.)

2. HOLLYWOOD SIGN, atop Mt. Lee

The Hollywood Sign, which may be more recognizable worldwide than the Statue of Liberty or the White House, is actually a giant billboard with letters over fifty feet high and thirty feet wide. It was originally constructed in 1923 as "Hollywoodland" to advertise homes sold by the Hollywoodland Realty Company (still in existence in Beachwood Canyon). When the last four letters of "Hollywoodland" fell off into disrepair and were removed, the sign became a symbol of the entertainment industry itself.

Until recently, it was possible to hike to the sign from Mulholland Highway, which provides close-up views. However, a gate has since been erected to discourage vandals and jumps by the potentially suicidal.

Photo ops: The sign can be photographed from a number of sites in and around Hollywood. News magazines like "Entertainment Tonight" often set up their cameras in a dirt patch next to Castillo del Lago. To reach the site from Hollywood, take the Hollywood Freeway north to the Barham exit and turn right. Turn right again on Lake Hollywood. After going up and down a hill, turn left on Tahoe Drive and then right on Canyon Lake. Park across the street from a soccer field and walk up the hill to take pictures.

Castillo del Lago, once owned by Madonna and Bugsy Siegel.

The famous chase scene in the original *Invasion of the Body Snatchers* was filmed just outside Hollywoodland Realty.

3. WOLF'S LAIR, 2869 Durand Drive

Efrem Zimbalist, Jr., and Doris Day are former tenants of this intriguing chateau, situated at the end of the hiking trail alongside Castillo del Lago.

The house was featured in the 1978 film *Return from Witch Mountain*, starring Bette Davis. Its original owner, Milton Wolf, a developer who designed the fairy tale-looking turrets, towers, and ramparts, died at the dining room table, leading to tales that this is one of L.A.'s many haunted houses.

4. "INVASION OF THE BODY SNATCHERS" CHASE SITE, corner Belden and Beachwood Drives

While some of the most memorable scenes in the original *Invasion of the Body Snatchers* (1955) were filmed in the town square of Sierra Madre, a small community just northeast of Pasadena (it was there that Kevin McCarthy and Dana Wynter hid from the pod people), the scenes of their escape were filmed at the corner of Beachwood and Belden Drives. The couple ran eastward up the hill on Belden Drive, and then up a flight of 148 steps actually located one block north of that intersection, at the corner of Beachwood and Woodshire Drives.

The area is one of the most intriguing in Hollywood, and do not be surprised if you see familiar artistic faces in the Beachwood Market at 2701 Belden Drive or the Village Coffee Shop two doors away.

5. BRONSON CAVES (at the end of Canyon Drive)

The Klingon prison camp in *Star Trek VI;* the Bat Cave in both the TV series "Batman" and the first feature film of the same name; the antediluvian village in *The Scorpion King;* the jungle island in the original *King Kong;*

and numerous gunfights on "Gunsmoke," "Bonanza," and "Have Gun, Will Travel," were all filmed here.

The caves are considered part of Griffith Park, but are not reachable through the park's main entrance. To see the caves, take Canyon Drive north until it ends, and hike a quarter of a mile up the trail to the right of the last parking lot.

6. CASTLE FORMERLY OWNED BY NICOLAS CAGE, 5647 Tryon Road

Cage lived in this 5,367-square-foot castle overlooking downtown L.A. between 1990 and 2000. The Academy-Award- winning actor has at various times owned another castle in Ireland, a Victorian house in San Francisco, an oceanfront home in Malibu, Tom Jones' old home in Bel Air, and, believe it or not, an apartment near Skid Row in downtown Los Angeles "so I can pretend I'm living incognito in some South American country."

7. AMERICAN FILM INSTITUTE, 2021 N. Western Avenue (north of Franklin Avenue)

Established in 1967, the American Film Institute is a prestigious nonprofit national arts organization devoted to preserving film and encouraging new talent. Its Center for Advanced Film and Television Studies offers specialized postgraduate training in producing, directing, screenwriting, cinematography and production design.

8. GRIFFITH PARK OBSERVATORY, 2800 E. Observatory Road, (323) 664-1191

Griffith Park—which is the largest urban park in the United States—is sometimes referred to as an unofficial Hollywood back lot since so many productions are filmed there. Says the park's film coordinator: "When companies need green space or a road that doesn't have buildings on it, they come here."

Blast-off scenes in *The Rocketeer* (1991); the final fight scenes in *Rebel Without a Cause* (1955); the opening scenes of *The Terminator* (1984), in which Arnold Schwarzenegger traveled back in time; and the supposed demise of Charlie's Angels in *Charlie's Angels II: Full Throttle* (2002), were filmed at the park observatory. A bust of James Dean stands on the planetarium's west front lawn.

9. LOS ANGELES ZOO, 5333 Zoo Drive, (323) 666-4090

Seen in opening credits of the 1977-84 ABC sitcom "Three's Company" and the feature films *Dragnet* (1987) and *Eraser* (1996).

10. ENNIS-BROWN HOUSE, 2655 Glendower Avenue

In the 1991 feature *Grand Canyon*, Steve Martin's character, an obnoxious producer, lived in this architecturally historic house, which was designed by Frank Lloyd Wright to resemble a Mayan temple.

The Ennis-Brown House was also featured in 1992's *Blade Runner* (the exterior served as Harrison Ford's home), *Rush Hour* (1998), *House on Haunted Hill* (1958), *Karate Kid III* (1989), and *Black Rain* (1989). It was also depicted as the mansion where Angel (David Boreaz) lived in the 1997–2003 WB TV series "Buffy the Vampire Slayer." Tours of the Ennis-Brown House are conducted thrice weekly. For hours and prices call (323) 660-0607.

What appears to be a castle at 2818 Hollyridge Drive (at the corner of Pelham) is actually a false front to a conventional hillside home. Down the street, though, at 3030 Hollyridge Drive, is a real castle that can be seen from the street.

The Griffith Park Observatory.

11. ANOTHER FORMER MADONNA HOME, 4519 Cockerham Drive

After she moved out of Castillo del Lago, Madonna lived in a 5,000-square foot Mediterranean-style mansion here, just west of Vermont Avenue. This was her home between 1996 and 2000. Madonna later sold the house to Jenna Elfman, who in turn sold it to Katey Sagal, who sold it to a noncelebrity. The house, which is behind gates, is not visible from the street.

NOT ON THE MAP—and down the street from a faux castle at 2818 Hollyridge Drive—is the home of Robert Pastorelli, the actor best known as "Murphy Brown"'s eccentric painter, Eldin. Pastorelli died there—at 2751 Hollyridge Drive—on March 8, 2004, of a heroin overdose. At the time of his death he was the prime suspect in the reopened investigation of the 1999 gunshot killing of his girlfriend in the same house. Police had originally accepted Pastorelli's explanation that she accidentally killed herself. Five years later they reopened the investigation on the basis of information that still has not been made public.

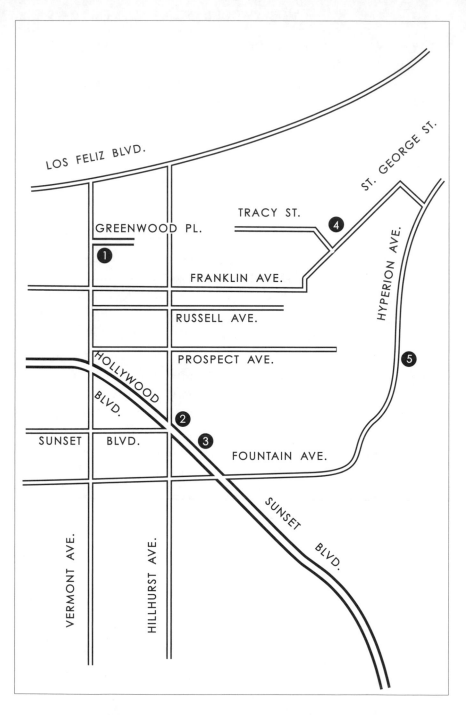

MAP 27   LOS FELIZ AND SILVER LAKE

LOS FELIZ AND SILVER LAKE

1. "MELROSE PLACE" APARTMENT BUILDING,
4616 Greenwood Place
Set designers added foliage to transform this
dumpy-looking apartment into the modern building seen on
the campy Fox-TV drama (1992-1999). Ironically, novelist
Raymond Chandler lived here in the early 1930s.

2. SITE OF "BABYLON," 4500 Sunset Boulevard
Although long gone, the largest outdoors movie set
ever built—the city of Babylon built for D. W. Griffith's 1916
silent film classic *Intolerance*—stood at this site for years.

3. KCET, 4401 Sunset Boulevard
One of the oldest continually used studios in
Hollywood. Allied Artists, Monogram Pictures, and other
long forgotten studios have made mostly "B" movies here
ever since 1912. Since 1971 the site has been occupied by
KCET, Southern California's public television station
(channel 28).
In *L.A. Story* (1991), KCET doubled as KYOY,
where Steve Martin played a daffy television weatherman.
Free one-hour tours are offered on Tuesdays and Thursdays.

4. JOHN MARSHALL HIGH SCHOOL, 3939 Tracy
Street
This high school was depicted as Rydell High School
in *Grease* (1978), Dason High in *Rebel Without a Cause*
(1955), Hemery High in the feature film *Buffy the Vampire*

Slayer (1992), Huntington Hills High in *Can't Hardly Wait* (1998), Pointes High in *Grosse Pointe Blank* (1997), and Jefferson High in the 1963-65 NBC drama "Mr. Novak."

Marshall alumni include "Catwoman" Julie Newman and Leonard DiCaprio, who graduated with the aid of a tutor. Hollywood madam Heidi Fleiss was a Marshall dropout.

5. SITE OF WALT DISNEY'S FIRST OFFICIAL STUDIO (1926-1940), 2701-39 Hyperion Avenue

A Gelson's grocery store now occupies the land where Mickey Mouse was created, and *Snow White and the Seven Dwarfs* (1938) was produced as the first feature-length animated film. In 1940, Disney moved his studios to Burbank. The site was declared a historic cultural monument by the city of Los Angeles in 1976.

The set of Babylon, which inspired the theme for Hollywood & Highland.

DOWNTOWN

1. DEPARTMENT OF WATER AND POWER, 111 N. Hope Street

The exterior of the DWP building was used as the 14th Precinct in the CBS crime show "Cagney and Lacey," (1982-1988) and Tacoma police headquarters in *Three Fugitives* (1989). The garage parking lot was used for shoot-out and chase scenes in *The Terminator* (1984).

2. DOROTHY CHANDLER PAVILION, 135 N. Grand Avenue, (213) 972-7211

The marble and black-glass Pavilion hosted 25 Academy Award presentations between 1969 and 1999. It is part of L.A.'s Music Center.

3. LOS ANGELES COUNTY COURTHOUSE, 111 N. Hill Street

4. CRIMINAL COURTS BUILDING, 210 W. Temple Street (at Broadway)

Site of O. J. Simpson's 1995 acquittal of double murder charges.

5. SECOND STREET TUNNEL (between Hill and Figueroa Streets)

Used frequently in movie chase scenes—including *The Terminator, Demolition Man, Godzilla,* and *Con Air.* For the *Independence Day* (1996) alien attack, the filmmakers and staged a huge traffic jam involving over

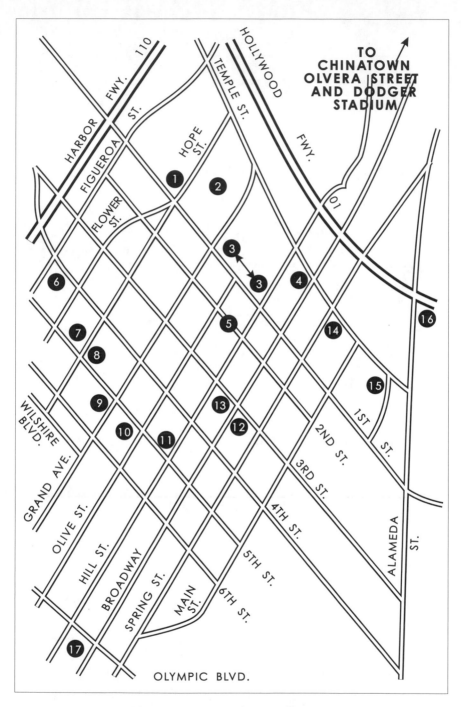

MAP 28 DOWNTOWN

300 cars, trucks, and buses. Wil Smith's girlfriend, played by Vivica A. Fox, narrowly escaped the fireball consuming downtown Los Angeles by kicking open a tunnel door, dragging her son and dog with her. In *Set It Off* (1996), the story of young black women who robbed banks for revenge against personal injustices, Fox and her partners-in-crime, Jada Pinkett and Queen Latifah, were trapped in the tunnel by the LAPD.

6. WESTIN BONAVENTURE HOTEL, 404 S. Figueroa Street, (213) 624-1000

In the 1993 feature *In The Line of Fire*, Clint Eastwood, playing an aging Secret Service agent assigned to protect the president, thwarted John Malkovich's assassination attempt here. The same glass elevator used for the climactic scene, in which Malkovich held Eastwood hostage, was also featured in one of the more memorable scenes in *True Lies* (1994). In that movie, Arnold Schwarzenegger, riding a horse he "borrowed" from a policeman, pursued a terrorist by galloping through the Bonaventure lobby, and continuing the pursuit on the elevator.

Assassins returned to the Bonaventure for the John Badham-directed *Nick of Time (*1995), this time for a plot against a liberal governor of California who was campaigning for re-election. Johnny Depp played a mild-mannered accountant who was sucked into the plot when Christopher Walken and Roma Maffia kidnapped his daughter and threatened to kill her unless Depp killed the governor. Bonaventure employees played heroic roles in thwarting that plot.

In a scene for *Rainman* (1988) filmed by the hotel's pool, Tom Cruise rejected a $250,000 bribe to return his autistic brother to an Ohio mental institution. The same pool collapsed and flooded the 30th floor beneath it in the Eddie Murphy DeNiro buddy comedy *Showtime* (2002). That movie contains a convincing shot of DeNiro and DeNiro dangling from the floor and about to be swept away off the building, until Murphy unconvincingly saved them both by handcuffing both of them to a supporting beam.

The frenetic shoot-out in *Heat* (1995) was filmed just outside the Bonaventure, at the corner of Fourth and Flower Streets.

The futuristic-looking Bonaventure has also been featured in *Strange Days, My Fellow Americans, Blue Thunder, Ruthless People, Mr. Mom, Virtuosity, The Poseidon Adventure,* and *Lethal Weapon 2.*

The hotel's BonaVista Lounge on the 35th floor was also where the daffy waitresses in the 1980s sitcom "It's a Living" worked.

7. "L.A. LAW" BUILDING, 444 S. Flower Street

While this building is best known as the building seen in TV's "L.A. Law," its offices have also been used for *Baby Boom* (1987), *Black Rain* (1989), *Beverly Hills Cop II* (1987), and *Gotcha!* (1985), where it served as CIA headquarters. The building was also used as the exterior of the bank Robert De Niro and Val Kilmer robbed in *Heat* (1995).

8. STANDARD HOTEL, 550 S. Flower Street

This hip hotel is the site of a popular nightspot frequented by young partygoers. It has also been in two movies. In 2005's film noir send-up *Kiss Kiss, Bang Bang,* Robert Downey, Jr., found a dead body in his room. In *Collateral* (2004) it appeared briefly in a scene in which a desperate Jamie Foxx stole a pedestrian's cell phone.

The futuristic Bonaventure Hotel.

The Biltmore Hotel.

9. THE U. S. BANK BUILDING (FORMERLY THE LIBRARY TOWER), 633 W. Fifth Street

Fittingly, this 75-story skyscraper—the tallest building west of the Mississippi—was where the aliens in *Independence Day* (1995) struck first, vaporizing flaky Angelinos who tried to stage a welcoming party on the building's rooftop.

In the less commercially successful film *Life Stinks* (1991), Mel Brooks had his offices here. Brooks played a developer who accepted a rival's challenge to try to survive for one month on Skid Row.

Tim Robbins's office in the 1997 *Nothing to Lose*, co-starring Matthew Lawrence, was also located here.

10. MILLENIUM BILTMORE HOTEL, 506 S. Grand Street (at Fifth Street), (213) 624-1011; in California (800) 252-0175

Since it opened in 1923, the Biltmore has hosted kings, presidents, Hollywood celebrities and virtually every major league baseball team. In 1960 John F. Kennedy set up the official headquarters for the Democratic National Convention in the Music Room (now the lobby), and it was here that JFK and his brother Bobby decided on Lyndon Baines Johnson as JFK's running mate. A few years later, the Beatles, who had been mobbed by fans during their first U.S. tour, secretly helicoptered to the hotel's rooftop and hid at the Biltmore until moving to another location.

Over the last 20 years at least 300 feature films, television programs, and commercials have been filmed at the hotel. In one of its most memorable appearances, Eddie Murphy conned his way into the hotel in *Beverly Hills Cop* (1984). Murphy later returned to the Biltmore to confront a potential research donor (James Coburn) in *The Nutty Professor* (1996). Ben Kingsley and his crew of alien-hunters chose the hotel as command central in *Species* (1995), and in *Splash* (1984) Darryl Hannah was unmasked as a mermaid in front of the hotel.

The Crystal Ballroom served as the setting for the bookie joint in *The Sting* (1973), the fight arena in *Rocky III* (1982), the prom scene in *Pretty in Pink* (1986), the banquet scene in *Alien Nation* (1979), the singing scenes in *The Fabulous Baker Boys* (1989), and the slime scenes in *Ghostbusters* (1984). *Vertigo* (1958) used the 11 flights of ornate, wrought-iron back stairs to create its dizzying scenes; and scenes from *Bugsy* (1991) and *The Fan* (1996) were filmed at the Biltmore Health Club. The hotel's other credits include *Independence Day, Romy and Michele's High School Reunion, True Lies, The American President, My Fellow Americans, Mother*, and *In The Line of Fire* (where it appeared as the hotel in Denver where Clint Eastwood and Rene Russo stayed.)

The Biltmore was also the setting of eight early Academy Award ceremonies: in 1931, 1935 through 1939, and 1941 and 1942. Actors Delta Burke and Gerald McRaney got married here in 1989.

11. GAS COMPANY TOWER, 555 Fifth Street (at Grand Street)

Directly across the street from the Biltmore is the 54-story office building featured in the opening scenes of *Speed* (1984). Keanu Reeves and Jeff Daniels rescued office workers trapped in a collapsing elevator.

The building was also depicted briefly as the federal office building where Jamie Foxx dropped off cab fare Jada Pinkett, and as the lobby of Pinkett's offices, in 2004's *Collateral*. It was not used, however, for any of the subsequent scenes in which Tom Cruise tried to kill her.

12. TITLE GUARANTEE AND TRUST BUILDING,
411 W. Fifth Street (at Hill Street, across from Pershing Square)

The exterior of this Art Deco building was depicted as the *Los Angeles Tribune* in the 1977-82 CBS drama "Lou Grant." Today the Spanish-language newspaper *La Opinion* has offices here.

13. BRADBURY BUILDING, 304 S. Broadway (at 3rd Street)

This historic building has been the setting of several television and movie private eye melodramas, including *Chinatown* (1974).

In *Blade Runner* (1982), Harrison Ford searched for androids here. In *Pay It Forward* (2001), Jay Mohr learned why a complete stranger gave him a Jaguar. The Bradbury also served as Jack Nicholson's publishing office in *Wolf* (1994), Christian Slater's law office in *Murder in the First* (1995), Dean Stockwell's detective office in *Mr. Wrong* (1996), and the offices of the *Los Angeles Sun* in Fox-TV's prime-time soap opera "Pasadena."

Sam Hall Kaplan, L.A.'s premier architectural critic, writes: "With its magical interior court bathed in light filtered through a glass roof and ornate ironwork and reflected off glazed yellow brick walls, the 1893 structure is one of the city's architectural treasures."

(Note: In this part of town, bring plenty of quarters to fend off the panhandlers.)

14. MILLION DOLLAR THEATER, 307 S. Broadway

This architecturally intriguing movie palace was built by showman Sid Grauman in 1917, five years before he built the Egyptian Theater in Hollywood and ten years before he built the Chinese Theater.

Los Angeles' City Hall.

The Shrine Auditorium.

15. CITY HALL, 200 N. Spring Street

"City Hall," writes *Los Angeles Times* researcher Cecilia Rasmussen, "has starred in more movies and television series than most Hollywood actors." Perhaps best known as the *Daily Planet* in the popular 1950s television series "Superman," City Hall, inside and out, has been seen in *48 Hours, Another 48 Hours, Die Hard II, Dragnet, Ricochet,* and *The Black Dahlia.* "Although it was destroyed by Martians in *War of the Worlds*," Rasmussen notes, "it somehow survived to portray the U.S. Capitol in 'The Jimmy Hoffa Story' and the Vatican in 'The Thorn Birds' . . . You might have caught a glimpse of City Hall in the series 'Kojak,' 'Cagney and Lacey,' 'The Rockford Files,' 'Matlock,' 'Hill Street Blues,' 'L.A. Law,' 'Equal Justice,' 'The Trials of Rosie O'Neill,' and 'The Big One: The Great Los Angeles Earthquake.'"

16. PARKER CENTER, 150 N. Los Angeles Street

Los Angeles Police Department headquarters. Seen in numerous television cop shows, most notably "Dragnet." The LAPD will be moving to new headquarters in the late 2000s.

17. UNION STATION, 800 N. Alameda Street, (213) 683-6987

Union Station has been featured in *Pearl Harbor, Grand Canyon, Blade Runner, Guilty by Suspicion, Bugsy, The Way We Were, Dear God, Nick of Time, Species,* several television series, and of course, the 1950 movie *Union Station* starring William Holden.

(Although there is a brief establishing shot of the station in 1976's *Silver Streak,* that movie was mostly filmed in Canada. The film required several stunts, and the station's management company does not grant filming permission to filmmakers who use on-site stunt work.)

18. HERALD EXAMINER BUILDING, 1111 S. Broadway

After the *Los Angeles Herald Examiner* went out of business in 1989, a location company moved in, and the building is now used exclusively as a location site for television shows and movies. In one of its more memorable roles, the building served as the L.A. police station where Kevin Spacey spun his tale of Keyser Soze in *The Usual Suspects* (1995).

The building itself, one of Los Angeles' most intriguing architectural landmarks, is being turned into condominiums and office space. It was designed by Julia Morgan, the pioneering architect whose design so pleased William Randolph Hearst that he commissioned her to build his oceanside mansion in Santa Monica and his castle at San Simeon.

JUST OFF THE MAP, at 1055 W. 7th St., is the Arco Tower, the building most often featured in Tom Cruise's hitman drama *Collateral* (2004). When Jamie Foxx sees Cruise in the building, he realizes Cruise is going to kill her. The interior scenes of Jada Pinkett's office were filmed here.

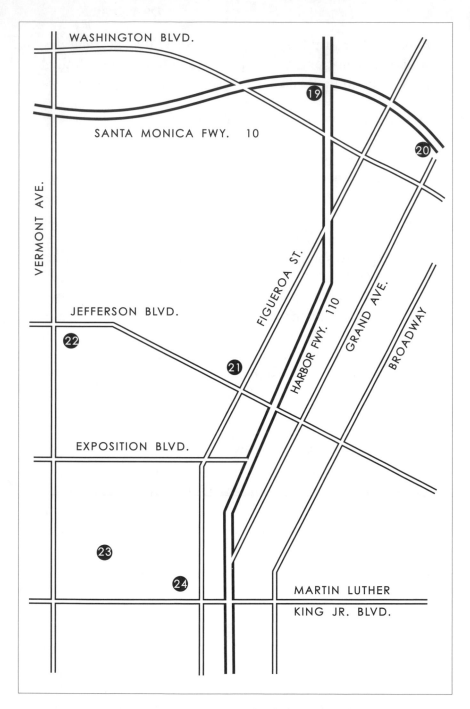

MAP 29 DOWNTOWN

19. "CHIPs" HEADQUARTERS, 777 W. Washington Boulevard

The exterior of the Central Los Angeles office of the California Highway Patrol was used in the 1977-1983 NBC action series "CHIPs."

20. OLYMPIC AUDITORIUM, 1801 S. Grand Avenue (south of 10 and east of 110)

Many of Sylvester Stallone's boxing scenes in the first three *Rocky* movies were filmed here.

21. SHRINE AUDITORIUM, 649 W. Jefferson Boulevard

The largest theater in the United States, the Shrine has been the site of ceremonies for the Academy Awards, the Grammys, the Emmys, the American Music Awards, and the MTV Awards. In the original *King Kong,* the gorilla was paraded in front of the auditorium and broke away from his chains. In *Naked Gun 33 1/3* (1994), Leslie Nielsen disrupted an Academy Awards ceremony while thwarting a terrorist plot. Goldie Hawn appeared from under a stage in *Foul Play* (1978), and extras danced bare-chested for Oliver Stone during a concert filmed for his movie *The Doors* (1991). The Shrine was also where Michael Jackson's hair caught on fire during the filming of a Pepsi commercial.

22. USC SCHOOL OF CINEMA AND TELEVISION, 850 W. 34 Street (by Jefferson Boulevard and McClintock Avenue)

USC, along with New York University, is widely considered to be the premier film school in the country. Its film school is modeled after a Hollywood studio, and includes sound stages, screening rooms, classrooms and administrative offices.

Alumni in the arts include *Star Wars* creator George Lucas; directors Ron Howard, Robert Zemeckis, and John Singleton; and actors LaVar Burton, Eric Close, Tate Donovan, Anthony Edwards, Will Ferrell, James Lesure, Tom Selleck, Marlo Thomas, and Forest Whitaker. John Wayne, Ron Howard, Macy Gray and sports legends Randy Johnson, Mark McGwire, Tom Seaver, and O. J. Simpson also attended USC.

Over 30 movies have been filmed on campus, including *Forrest Gump* (where it doubled for the University of Alabama), *The Graduate* (where it portrayed Berkeley), *Legally* Blonde and *The Paper Chase* (Harvard), *Orange County* (Stanford), *Blue Chips*, *Young Frankenstein, Rising Sun, Mr. Baseball*, and the 1939 classic *The Hunchback of Notre Dame,* which featured Notre Dame's Quasimado in the library's bell tower. USC also played the fictitious University of Northern California in Fox-TV's comedy "Undeclared."

23. LOS ANGELES MEMORIAL COLISEUM, 3911 S. Figueroa Street

The Coliseum is the only arena that has hosted two Olympic games (1932 and 1984), two Super Bowls (1967 and 1972), a World Series (1959), and a Papal visit (Pope John Paul II in 1987). The opening and closing scenes of *The Last Boy Scout* (1991) were filmed here, as were the climactic scenes in *Black Sunday* (1977) and the gladiatorial basketball scenes in *Escape from L.A.* (1996).

24. LOS ANGELES MEMORIAL SPORTS ARENA, 3939 S. Figueroa Street

Built in 1959, the Sports Arena hosts over 200 events each year. In 1960 John F. Kennedy was nominated for the presidency at the Democratic National Convention held here.

PASADENA

1. THE INCORRECTLY IDENTIFIED "BAT MANSION," 160 S. San Rafael Avenue (south of Colorado Avenue)

This extraordinary three-story Tudor mansion has been cited in other tour books as the house used as the Wayne Manor in the 1960s television series "Batman." However, Tonie Carnes, a researcher for the Pasadena Historical Society, discovered that the real Bat House was actually down the street a few blocks at 380 S. San Rafael Avenue.

160 S. San Rafael Avenue is not without its significance, though; it was used as Eddie Murphy's mansion in *Bowfinger* (1998), Sylvester Stallone's home in *Rocky V* (1990), and the house Harrison Ford tried to sell in *Hollywood Homicide* (2003).

The house was destroyed by fire in 1995, but you can still see the façade from the street.

2. THE REAL "BAT MANSION," 380 S. San Rafael Avenue

Unfortunately, the real Bat Mansion is not visible from the street. Neighbors say that the frequent filming at this mansion has sometimes created a carnival-like atmosphere on the street.

The house also served as Kenneth Branagh's home in *Dead Again* (1991), Brittany Murphy's home in *Just Married* (2003), and as Tim Curry's house of comedic horrors in *Scary Movie 2* (2001).

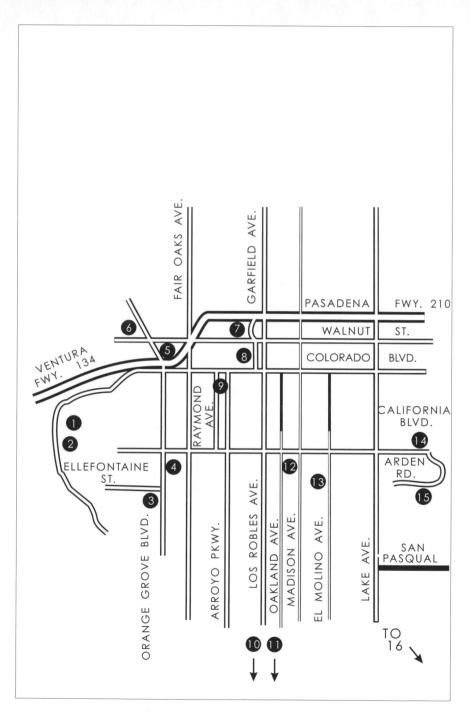

MAP 30 PASADENA

3. MAYFIELD SENIOR SCHOOL, 500 Bellafontaine Street

One of Pasadena's most popular location sites (mostly for television series, movies of the week, soap operas, and commercials), this private all-girls Catholic school was seen in *The Lost World* (where it served as Richard Attenborough's house), *The Nutty Professor* (the dean's office), The *Shadow* (Alec Baldwin's house), *Devil in a Blue Dress* (the foundation officers of Tom Sizemore), and *Newsies.*

Behind the school, on Bellafontaine Terrace, is the house seen in the TV sitcom "Valerie" starring Valerie Harper, in 1986. When Harper was replaced by Sandy Duncan the following year, the program became "Valerie's Family," and then "The Hogan Family," which aired on NBC, and then CBS, until 1990.

4. "DADDY DAY CARE CENTER," 351 Congress Place (east of Orange Grove)

In the 2003 comedy *Daddy Day Care*, Eddie Murphy and Jeff Garlin ran a day care center out of this Victorian home.

5. FENYES MANSION, 470 W. Walnut Street (corner of Orange Grove)

Now the permanent home of the Pasadena Historical Society, this mansion was one of two mansions used in Hal Ashby's 1979 feature *Being There.* (The other was the Cravens Estate at 430 Madeline Avenue—now the home of the Red Cross.)

In the movie, Peter Sellers played the ignorant caretaker whose silence was mistaken for profundity.

6. GAMBLE HOUSE, 4 Westmoreland Place (half a block north of the Fenyes Mansion, on a small, poorly marked side street just west of and reachable from the 300 block of Orange Grove Boulevard)

In the *Back to the Future* movies, Christopher Lloyd ("Doc") lived in this house. The house, built in 1908 for David and Mary Gamble of Procter & Gamble, is an internationally recognized architectural landmark, a product of the turn-of-the-century Arts and Crafts movement. For tour hours, call (626) 793-3334.

7. PASADENA PUBLIC LIBRARY, 285 E. Walnut Street

The library was Mara Wilson's hangout in *Matilda* (1996) and the San Francisco library in which Goldie Hawn worked in *Foul Play* (1978). In *Legally Blonde* (2001), it doubled for the Harvard Law Library, where Reese Witherspoon studied. In *Arachnophobia* (1990), Jeff Daniels researched insects here.

8. PASADENA CITY HALL, 100 N. Garfield Avenue

Used by the producers of the first two *Beverly Hills Cop* movies as the exterior of Beverly Hills City Hall. (Filming permits cost less in Pasadena than in Beverly Hills.) City Hall was also a French castle in *Patton* and a San Francisco courthouse in *Murder in the First.* The larger courtyard served as the site of Napa Valley's annual harvest festival and parade in *A Walk in the Clouds.*

9. CASTLE GREEN, 99 S. Raymond Avenue (corner of Green Street)

One of Pasadena's premier resort hotels before the turn of the century, the Castle Green condominium is a popular location site because of its unusual Middle Eastern architecture. The building was used as the Hotel Nacional de Cuba in *Bugsy*, the Austrian hotel where Steve Martin and Kathleen Turner honeymooned in *The Man with Two Brains*, a Russian consular office in San Francisco in *Sneakers*, a hospital morgue in the remake of *The Time Machine*, Tony Shaloub's hotel in *The Man Who Wasn't There*, and a restaurant in *The Marrying Man*. It was also where "the sting" took place in *The Sting*.

Public tours are conducted twice a year—usually in June and in December—by the Friends of the Castle Green and building's residents. For further information call the Castle Green at (626) 793-0359.

10. "BENSON MANSION," 1365 S. Oakland Avenue
The exterior of this house was used as the Governor's mansion on the popular sitcom "Benson," which aired on ABC from 1979 to 1986.

11. "BEVERLY HILLBILLIES" MOVIE HOUSE, 1288 S. Oakland Avenue (at Woodland)
Used for the exterior shots of the Clampett residence in *The Beverly Hillbillies* (1993) movie. Interior scenes were filmed in four different mansions in Beverly Hills. The house was also one of two homes featured as the Genovian Palace in *The Princess Diaries* (2001).

12. "DENNIS THE MENACE" HOUSE, 830 S. Madison Avenue
This was the house seen in the 1959-63 CBS sitcom "Dennis the Menace," starring Jay North.

13. "FATHER OF THE BRIDE" HOUSE, 843 S. El Molino Avenue
Although the 1991 remake of *Father of the Bride* identified Steve Martin and Diane Keaton's residence as

The Gamble House.

William A. Gordon (left) and former owner Charles Morton at the oft-filmed "Dynasty Mansion."

being located in San Marino, the house was actually located in Pasadena, a few blocks north of San Marino (which discourages filmmaking by making their permits to be more expensive). The producers considered the house more expensive). The producers considered the house almost a character in the story. They looked for a house in an old-fashioned, idealized community—and considered this white clapboard residence perfect.

14. CALIFORNIA INSTITUTE OF TECHNOLOGY, 1200 E. California Boulevard (between Hill and Wilson Avenues)

Caltech would rather be known for its inventions (the seismograph and Richter scale); its scientific discoveries (anti-matter, quasars, quarks, and the nature of the chemical bond); its illustrious faculty and alumni (29 Nobel Laureates and counting); and its consistent ranking as one of the top research universities in the world.

Of course, since it is so close to Hollywood, Caltech occasionally shows up on the silver screen. The Athenaeum—a faculty dining club originally conceived as a meeting place for scholars—appeared in *Beverly Hills Cop* (1984) as the private club Eddie Murphy conned his way into, resulting in a fight in which Murphy threw Jonathan Banks across a buffet table. Caltech also appeared as David Krumholz's college in CBS's "Numbers." In movies it has made appearances in *Legally Blonde, The Wedding Planner, Orange County, Starship Troopers, Real Genius, The War of the Roses, Funny About Love*, and *The Witches of Eastwick*.

15. "THE CARRINGTON MANSION," 1145 Arden Road

This is not the house seen in the opening credits of "Dynasty" (that one is located in the San Francisco suburb of Woodside). It is, however, the one that was used for the garden and pool shots (including Joan Collins' famous fights with Linda Evans) and for close-up outdoor scenes with the actors.

The 20,000-square-foot mansion, Arden Villa, has been a frequent filming site, dating back to the 1933 Marx Brothers' classic *Duck Soup*. According to Charles Morton, a former owner who handled filming and corporate affair rentals at the mansion, Arden Villa has appeared in at least 200 productions between 1980 and 2000, including four television movies about the Kennedys, "Nixon's Last Days," several episodes of "Hart to Hart," "Flamingo Road," Eddie Murphy's *The Distinguished Gentleman* (1992) and Charles Bronson's *Death Wish* (1974). The house also was one of several used as the Cleary mansion in *The Wedding Crashers* (2006), and the Knight Rider Foundation in the 1982-86 NBC adventure series "Knight Rider."

The Walsh family home on "Beverly Hills 90210" is actually located at 1675 East Altadena Drive in Altadena, about four miles northeast of downtown Pasadena and a good forty minutes' drive from Beverly Hills. Down the street, at 1605 Altadena Drive, is the house depicted as Luke Perry's on the show.

16. THE HUNTINGTON LIBRARY, ART COLLECTIONS, AND BOTANICAL GARDENS, 1151

Oxford Road, San Marino, (626) 405-2100

This museum features 18th and 19th century British and French art, American art from the 1730s to the 1930s, rare books and manuscripts, and 150 acres of botanical gardens.

Its grounds have been featured in numerous movies, including the Dermot Mulroney-Cameron Diaz nuptials in *My Best Friend's Wedding* (1997); Catherine Zeta-Jones' marriage to Billy Bob Thornton in *Intolerable Cruelty* (2003); and the Adam Sandler-Drew Barrymore union in *The Wedding Singer* (1998). All three filmed on the North Vista.

In *Memoirs of a* Geisha (2005), an artificial 30-foot-tall cherry tree was built in the Japanese Garden, where Ziyi Zhang went to attend a Cherry Blossom Festival. The East Coast monastery that Jack Nicholson took Adam Sandler to in *Anger Management* (2003) also featured this garden, although the main set was built in the Lily Pond area.

The Huntington's Conservatory was the site of Allyson Hanigan and Jason Biggs' wedding in *American Wedding* (2003). *The Good German* (2006) was filmed in the Huntington Gallery (during a period when all the art had been removed and the building was about to undergo restoration); and the same gallery was portrayed as Robert Redford's mansion in *Indecent Proposal* (1993); the Halloween party site in *A Cinderella Story* (2004), a country club in *Starsky & Hutch* (2004), and an exclusive girl's school in *Be Cool* (2005). The Mausoleum was featured as a Washington, D.C. dog park in *Legally* Blonde 2 (2003), although Reese Witherspoon's wedding took place in the Rose Garden.

Other movies that have filmed on the grounds include *Monster-in-Law* (2005), *Serenity* (2005), *The Nutty Professor* (1996), *Beverly Hills Ninja* (1997), *Coming to America* (1988), *Master of Disguise* (2002), *First Daughter* (2004), *The Wedding Planner* (2001), and *Scavenger Hunt* (1979).

OTHER PASADENA FILM SITES:

• A house at 1565 San Pasqual (east of Lake Street) was used for exterior shots of *Mr. and Mrs. Smith* (2005). Another house was used for the interior gunfights between Brad Pitt and Angelina Jolie.

• The movie *Dangerous Minds* and the NBC-TV series "American Dreams" both filmed at Washington Middle School , 1505 N. Marengo.

• Rose City High School (323 S. Oak Knoll) was featured as Tobey Maguire and Reese Witherspoon's high school in Gary Ross' directorial debut *Pleasantville*.

• The Ritz-Carlton Hotel & Spa (1440 S. Oak Knoll) was one of the locations that depicted the San Francisco hotel where Lindsay Lohan, playing identical twins, tried to bring together her parents in the 1998 remake of *The Parent Trap*. *Seabiscuit* was also filmed there.

JUST OFF THE MAP, in South Pasadena, are a number of other homes featured in movies and television series. The house that Ken Olin and Mel Harris supposedly lived in on "thirtysomething"—which we were told was in Philadelphia—was actually located at 1710 Bushnell Avenue in South Pasadena. Owner Donna Potts told a reporter that a location scout just came to the door one day before filming began and later offered a contract to the family.

The house directly across the street—at 1711 Bushnell—was both the 1955 house where Lea Thompson and her family took in Michael J. Fox in *Back to the Future* (1985), and Fox's home in *Teen Wolf* (1985).

In the *Back to the Future* series, 1711 served as Crispin Glover's home, 1705 as Elisabeth Shue's, and 1809 as Thomas Wilson's. 1621 and 1615 Bushnell were both used as Bill Cosby's home in *Ghost Dad* (1990).

One block west, at 1632 Fletcher, is Patricia Wettig and Tim Busfield's house in "thirtysomething."

Another block west of that is Milan Avenue, where Charles Grodin lived in 1992's *Beethoven* (at 1405). The house in the 1976-80 ABC series "Family" is on the 600 block of Milan.

In South Pasadena's historic business district is Carrows Restaurant (815 S. Fremont Avenue), where Linda Hamilton, playing Sarah Connor, waitressed in *The Terminator* (1984).

Down the street, at 1518 Mission Street, is L. L. Balk Hardware—the hardware store where Fox worked at in *Teen Wolf* (1985).

Around the corner from L. L. Balk is the Rialto Theater, at 1023 S. Fair Oaks Avenue. It was at the Rialto that Tim Robbins, playing a studio executive in Robert Altman's feature *The Player* (1992), met Vincent

D'Onofrio, who played the writer whom Robbins thought was sending him threatening postcards. In the movie Robbins killed D'Onofrio behind the theater.

Jim Carrey's house in *Liar, Liar* (2003)—at 1004 Highland—is just west of Fremont at 1004 Highland St.

Also off the map—in the western section of Pasadena (just north of the Gamble House and south of the Rose Bowl)—is Brookside Park. In *High Anxiety* (1987), Mel Brooks paid homage to Alfred Hitchcock's classic *The Birds* by filming a scene there in which he was drenched by bird droppings.

Not far from the park, at 1090 Nithsdale Rd., is San Rafael Elementary School, which has appeared in two Jim Carrey movies. In "Liar, Liar" (1997), Carrey visited his son at the school. In "Bruce Almighty" (2003), Carrey's girlfriend Jennifer Aniston taught at the school.

Between Pasadena and Glendale is the community of Eagle Rock, home of Occidental College. The college played California University in the hit TV series "Beverly Hills 90210."

Glendale is also the childhood hood of legend John Wayne. All but one of his childhood homes have been torn down. The Glendale Pharmacy where he worked as a soda jerk was located on the site that is now a Borders Books & Music.

The Queen Anne cottage seen in the television series "Fantasy Island" is located at the Arboretum of Los Angeles County, at 301 N. Baldwin Avenue in Arcadia, no more than a ten-minute drive southeast of downtown Pasadena. The Arboretum is a 127-acre botantical park which features exotic trees and shrubs arranged by their continent of origin. The opening sequence of "Fantasy Island" included stock footage of an airplane landing on the lake and Herve Villechaise's character, Tatoo, ringing the bell in the cottage tower, yelling "De plane, de plane." The producers actually only filmed a few episodes at the Arboretum, and then constructed a replica on the studio lot. The Arboretum has appeared in well over 200 television episodes and films, including eight Tarzan movies, *The African Queen, The Road to Singapore, The Lost World, Anaconda,* and other movies with jungle settings. Although unrecognizable (because it was painted brown), It was also Barbra Streisand and Dustin Hoffman's home in *Meet the Fockers.* For hours, call (626) 821-3222.

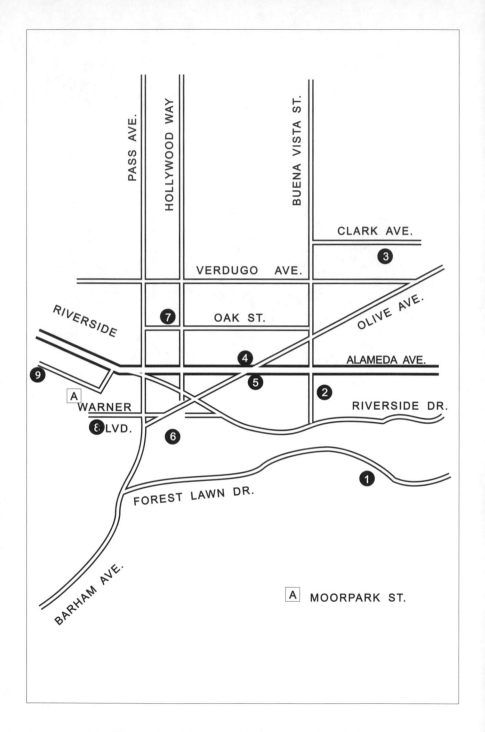

MAP 31 BURBANK AND TOLUCA LAKE

BURBANK AND
TOLUCA LAKE

1. FOREST LAWN MEMORIAL PARK HOLLY-WOOD HILLS, 6300 Forest Lawn Drive

This huge cemetery is the final resting place of Gene Autry; Lucille Ball; Bette Davis; Sammy Davis, Jr.; Andy Gibb; Buster Keaton; Stan Laurel; Liberace; Ozzie, Harriet, and Ricky Nelson; Freddie Prinze; George Raft; John Ritter; Gene Roddenberry; McLean Stevenson; and Jack Webb. Park maps are available at the front gates, but they do not show the locations of the stars' graves. A book, *Hollywood Remains to Be Seen* by Mark J. Masek, does. That book also covers celebrity graves at Forest Lawn Glendale, 1712 S. Glendale Avenue, where many other luminaries are buried and where Ronald Reagan married Jane Wyman on January 26, 1940, at the Wee Kirk o' the Heather Church.

2. DISNEY STUDIOS, 500 S. Buena Vista Street

Since 1940, this has been the headquarters of Disney Studios, a company whose movies are loved by children—and whose tight-fisted business dealings are less loved by writers, producers and agents. In an article for *Vanity Fair*, journalist Peter J. Boyer called Disney "a place so reviled that even its architecture inspires nasty rumors, such as the apocryphal story that architect Michael Graves arranged the drainage system in the Disney headquarters building in such a way that the huge sculpted Seven Dwarfs

231

atop the edifice would seem to be peeing on Disney executives whenever it rained." Boyer also called Disney "a place so tough in its dealings with the outside, so rigidly demanding of its own people, that it has earned an unlovely nickname that will be hard to erase. They call it Mouschwitz."

Of course, those who run Disney know that most people will not care how they treat the people who work with or for them, and will more likely associate Disney with its wonderful fairy tale movies such as *Snow White and the Seven Dwarfs, The Little Mermaid, Beauty and the Beast, Alladin, 101 Dalmations*, and *The Lion King* as well as its famous television shows: "Zorro," "Dragnet," and "The Wonderful World of Disney." The studio, apparently not wishing to compete with Disneyland, does not offer a tour of its facilities.

The Disney administration building.

3. BURROUGHS HIGH SCHOOL, 1920 Clark Avenue

One of the high schools used in the filming of ABC's Emmy Award-winning comedy-drama "The Wonder Years." Alumni include Debbie Reynolds, Ron Howard, and Rene Russo. While promoting *Ransom*, directed by Howard and co-starring Russo, the actress repeatedly told reporters how she used to cheat off Howard during tests. Russo was a Burroughs dropout.

4. DICK CLARK PRODUCTIONS, 3003 W. Olive Avenue

These are the offices of Clark's production company, which produces the American Music Awards, the Golden Globe Awards, the Academy of Country Music Awards, "New Year's Rockin' Eve," movies made for television, and game shows. No tours.

(Note: If you have ever wanted to take a side trip to beautiful downtown Burbank, just take Olive Avenue north. It has been revitalized since Johnny Carson joked about it in his monologues.

The house featured in the "The Wonder Years" is just northwest of downtown at 516 University Avenue.)

5. NBC STUDIOS, 3000 W. Alameda Avenue

At $8.50 for adults, $7.50 for seniors, and $5.00 for children 5 to12, the NBC tour is the best bargain in town. Call (818) 840-3537 for hours and information. That number is also good for ticket information to see a taping of "The Tonight Show" and other shows filmed at the studio. The studio's ticket counter opens at 8:00 A.M. and distributes tickets for shows that tape for that evening. Ticket requests are also honored by mail if you write to the studio with the name of the show and enclose a self-addressed stamped envelope.

NBC Studios in Burbank.

An aerial view of Warner Bros.

6. WARNER BROS. STUDIOS, 4000 Warner Boulevard

Warner Bros., which has been headquarted here since 1929, offers a two-hour tour of its back lot and studio facilities. The tour, Warner spokespersons point out, "is not a charade created for mass audiences, but is, in fact, designed for small groups—no more than 12 persons—so that they may learn about the various components that go into the making of a film."

Since each tour guide is allowed to customize his or her own tour, and activity on the lot changes daily, no two tours are identical. However, all stop by the new Warner Bros. Museum and visit the back lot sets where hundreds of feature films and episodic television shows have been filmed over the years. Tourists are allowed to wander around some of these sets and take pictures, provided that they are not being used for upcoming productions.

Seeing a television show or feature being filmed on the back lot is not guaranteed, but it is a common occurrence. No one under eight is admitted. For prices and hours call (818) 972-TOUR.

7. WARNER BROS. RANCH FACILITIES, 3701 W. Oak Street

Behind the walls of this 40-acre back lot are sound stages and movie sets used in countless movies. The streets include the facade of "Murphy Brown"'s townhouse, the houses from "Bewitched," "I Dream of Jeannie," and "The Partridge Family," Danny Glover's house in *Lethal Weapon 2* (1989), Kevin Spacey and Annette Bening's house in *American Beauty* (1999), and Garp's house in *The World According to Garp* (1982). The back lot is only sometimes shown during the Warner Bros. tour and is not otherwise open to the public.

8. "SCARECROW AND MRS. KING" HOUSE, 4247 Warner Boulevard

The exterior of this Cape Cod was used as Kate Jackson and Beverly Garland's home in the 1983-87 CBS adventure series "Scarecrow and Mrs. King."

9. LONGTIME HOME OF BOB HOPE, 10346 Moorpark Street

The comedian bought this white-brick, 15-room house in 1940.

CELEBRITIES WHO LIVE IN TOLUCA LAKE include Scott Baio, Kirsten Dunst, Andy Garcia, Jennifer Love Hewitt, Wayne Knight, George Lopez, Garry Marshall, Markie Post, Alan Thicke, Robert Urich, Damon Wayans, Jonathan Winters, and Joanne Worley.

Former residents include Bing Crosby, who originally lived at 4326 Forman Ave., and then moved to a house at 10500 Camarillo Street, a home that was subsequently owned by Andy Griffith and later by Jerry Van Dyke; W. C. Fields; Moe Howard; Al Jolson; Freddie Prinze, Jr.; (who lived next door to Bob Hope); Frank Sinatra; and Henry Winkler.

Denzel Washington lived at 4701 Sancola Avenue between 1992 and 1999. William Holden once owned that house and hosted his friends Ronald and Nancy Reagan's 1952 wedding party there.

According to *Letters from Amelia*, famed aviator Amelia Earhart bought the house at the very end of Valley Spring Lane, across from Lakeside Country Club, in 1935, two years before she mysteriously disappeared while trying to fly around the world.

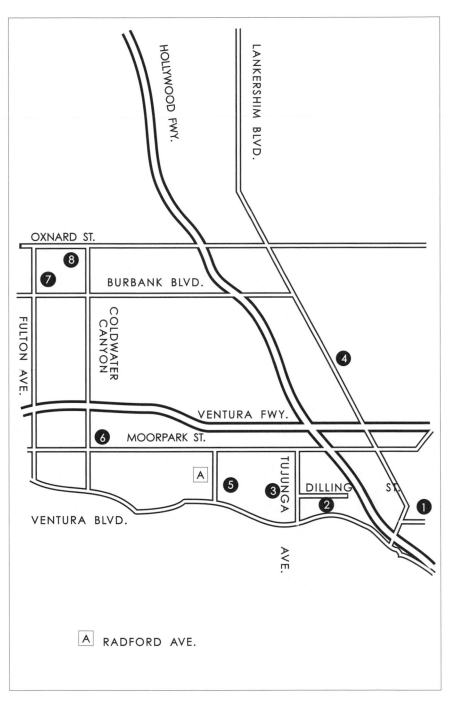

MAP 32 UNIVERSAL CITY, NORTH HOLLYWOOD, & STUDIO CITY

Filming on the Universal Studios backlot.

UNIVERSAL CITY, NORTH HOLLYWOOD AND STUDIO CITY

1. UNIVERSAL STUDIOS HOLLYWOOD, 100 Universal City Plaza, (818) 508-9600

As a tourist attraction, Universal Studios Hollywood ranks second in Southern California only to Disneyland. In fact, it is so popular that the theme park actually makes more money every year for NBC Universal than its movies.

Universal offers stunt shows, technical attractions, rides, and a narrated tram tour through Universal's back lot, the largest in the world. The Bates Motel, seen in *Psycho,* is there, as are the sets used in *Back to the Future* (the Hill Valley courthouse), *The Sting,* and quite a few homes from Universal television series, including "Murder She Wrote," "Matlock," "Leave It To Beaver," and "The Munsters," as well as Wisteria Lane from "Desperate Housewives." Other highlights include a museum dedicated to Lucille Ball and "Jurassic Park—The Ride," which is particularly popular when temperatures in the San Fernando Valley soar during summertime. Tourists emerge from the ride happily drenched.

Adjacent to the park is Universal City Walk, a three-block-long entertainment and shopping promenade that has become a popular local and tourist destination in and of itself. City Walk features entertainment-themed restaurants and shops, a complex of theaters, and one-of-a-kind specialty stores.

2. "THE BRADY BUNCH" HOUSE, 11222 Dilling Street

House used for the exterior of the popular ABC sitcom, which aired from 1969 to 1974. Because a new fence altered the house's appearance, and the new owner refused offers of cash to tear it down, the producers of the movie version did not return here for filming. Instead, they built a facade replicating the house around another house on Firmament Avenue in Sherman Oaks.

3. ACADEMY OF TELEVISION ARTS AND SCIENCES, 5220 Lankershim Boulevard (corner of Magnolia Boulevard)

Closed to the general public. Outside the building is a Hall of Fame Plaza featuring bronze statutes of Lucille Ball, Jack Benny, Mary Tyler Moore, and other members of the Academy's Hall of Fame.

4. VITELLO'S RESTAURANT, 4349 Tujunga Avenue, (818) 769-0905

On May 4, 2001, actor Robert Blake's wife, 44-year-old Bonny Lee Bakley, ate her last meal here shortly before she was murdered. Bakley was sitting alone in the couple's car, parked a block away, when a gunman fired at her through the passenger's window.

Blake's alibi—that he left his wife alone in their car while he returned to the restaurant to retrieve a gun he left behind—never made any sense. The subsequent trashing of Bakley's character by Blake's attorney and revelations about their unhappy marriage only served to deepen suspicions that the actor may have played some role in Bakley's death. Blake was subsequently indicted on one count of murder and two counts of soliciting murder, but acquitted on March 16, 2005. Later that year, a civil jury ruled that Blake "intentionally caused" Bakley's death (without determining whether he pulled the trigger himself) and awarded her children $30 million in damages.

5. FIRST CHRISTIAN CHURCH. 4390 Colfax Avenue (at the corner of Moorpark Street)

In the 1996-2007 WB series "7th Heaven," this church was depicted as the Glen Oaks Community Church. Stephen Collins played Reverend Eric Camden, the pastor.

6. HOME OF THE *40 YEAR OLD VIRGIN*, 12016 Moorpark Street

In the 2005 comedy Steve Carrell supposedly lived in Apartment 5.

7. CBS STUDIO CENTER, 4024 Radford Avenue

This studio has changed hands several times since Mack Sennett, "The King of Comedy," built it in 1928. It has variously been Mascot Pictures, Republic Studios, CBS Television Center, CBS/Fox Studios and CBS/MTM.

Many of the most memorable programs in television history have been produced here: "Rawhide," "Gunsmoke," "The Mary Tyler Moore Show," "The Bob Newhart Show," "Rhoda," "Lou Grant," "WKRP in Cincinnati," "Gilligan's Island," "The Wild, Wild West," "My Three Sons," "Hawaii Five-0," "Get Smart," "Hill St. Blues," "St. Elsewhere," "Remington Steele," "Falcon Crest," "Roseanne," "Cybill," "Third Rock From the Sun," "Malcolm in the Middle," and "Seinfeld."

No tours; no visitors allowed.

8. LITTLE BROWN CHURCH IN THE VALLEY, 4418 Coldwater Canyon

Ronald Reagan and second wife Nancy Davis were married here on March 4, 1952.

9. LOS ANGELES VALLEY COLLEGE, 5800 Fulton Avenue

Danny DeVito took writing classes from Billy Crystal here in the 1987 black comedy *Throw Momma From the Train.*

10. GRANT HIGH SCHOOL, 13000 Oxnard Street (at Coldwater Canyon)

Used for the filming of *Clueless* (1995), which starred Alicia Silverstone, and teen-oriented TV shows, including "The Wonder Years," "Beverly Hills 90210," and "Life Goes On."

Alumni include Tom Selleck, Brian Robbins, Mickey Dolenz, Rob Beck, and Mitch Gaylord.

JUST OFF THE MAP—at 12334 Cantura Street— is the dinky two-bedroom bungalow featured in the Fox-TV sitcom "Malcolm in the Middle." When the house was offered for sale in the mid-1990s (at a then mind-blowing $479,000), a Studio City realtor told *Entertainment Weekly*: "The house has its own income. They (the producers) pay about $3,000 to $4,000 a day" for the rights to film there. Overall, the owners reportedly earned over $100,000 renting out the house.

CELEBRITIES WHO OWN HOMES IN STUDIO CITY include Elayne Boosler, William Daniels and Bonnie Bartlett, Shelley Duvall, Erik Estrada, Lucy Lawless, Michael McDonald, Michael J. McKean, Alyssa Milano, Jay North, William Shatner, Betty Thomas, and George Wendt.

SHERMAN OAKS, VAN NUYS, AND ENCINO

1. MARILYN MONROE'S FIRST HONEYMOON HOME, 4524 Vista del Monte (one block west of Van Nuys Boulevard)

After marrying her first husband, Jim Dougherty, on June 19, 1942, a 16-year-old Norma Jean Baker (who later changed her name to Marilyn Monroe) lived in a one-room studio apartment here for a few months.

2. VAN NUYS HIGH SCHOOL, 6535 Cedros Avenue

One of the high schools used for the filming of "The Wonder Years" and "Life Goes On." *Fast Times at Ridgemont High* and *My Science Project* were also shot here.

Famous alumni include Robert Redford, Don Drysdale, Natalie Wood, Paula Abdul, Stacy Keach, and Jane Russell. Marilyn Monroe attended school here for a year, but was not graduated.

3. SHERMAN OAKS GALLERIA, 15303 Ventura Boulevard

Moon Unit Zappa spoofed this once-notorious teen hangout—and the spoiled, cliquish teen-agers she met at Bar Mitzvah parties—in her hit song "Valley Girls." The Galleria was also the site of the filming of *Fast Times at*

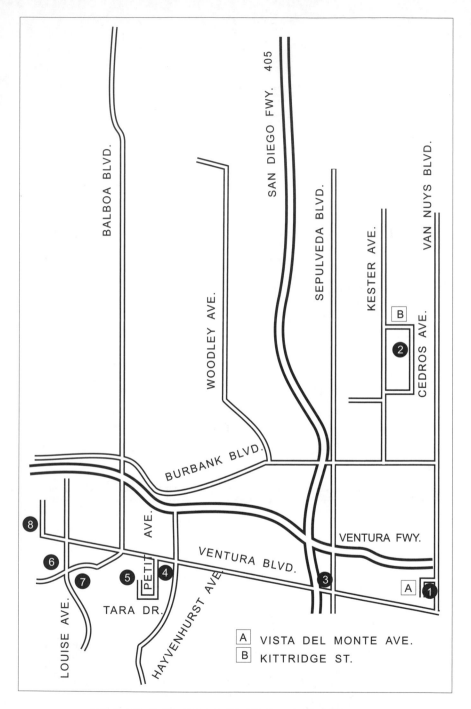

BALBOA BLVD.

SAN DIEGO FWY. 405

SEPULVEDA BLVD.

WOODLEY AVE.

KESTER AVE.

VAN NUYS BLVD.

B

2

CEDROS AVE.

BURBANK BLVD.

8

6

PETIT AVE.

VENTURA FWY.

7

5

4

VENTURA BLVD.

LOUISE AVE.

TARA DR.

HAYVENHURST AVE.

3

A

1

A   VISTA DEL MONTE AVE.
B   KITTRIDGE ST.

MAP 33 SHERMAN OAKS,
VAN NUYS & ENCINO

Ridgemont High, Commando, and according to one mall official, "a lot of B movies we'd rather not talk about."

In 1999, the mall closed and was transformed into an office complex. It is now the headquarters of Warner Bros.'s animation studios.

4. FORMER HOME OF MICHAEL JACKSON, 4641 Hayvenhurst Avenue

The self-anointed King of Pop moved to the 2,700-acre Neverland Ranch in Santa Barbara in 1988, but this 8,000-square-foot home, where his parents and at least one of his brothers have resided since 1971, is still listed in his name. *Entertainment Weekly* reports that "a metal star engraved with his name is embedded in the walkway to the 20-room mansion, lest anyone forget that this is a house that Michael built and still maintains."

In 1993 Los Angeles police officers, investigating allegations that Michael molested young boys, raided the home and seized several boxes of items from his old bedroom.

5. "HOUSE OF TWO GABLES," 4543 Tara Drive

Gable lived here with three of his wives: Carole Lombard, Lady Sylvia Ashley and Kay Williams Spreckles. In 1977 the home was purchased by Michael R. Milken.

6. MANSION PREVIOUSLY OWNED BY KIRSTIE ALLEY AND AL JOLSON, 4875 Louise Avenue

During her 13-year marriage to Parker Stevenson, Alley lived in what Barbara Walters called "one of the loveliest homes I've ever seen." We do not know if she kept her promise, but according to Walters, Kirstie vowed to spend $400 a week on flowers in the home—the amount she used to spend for cocaine. Previous owners include Al Jolson, who originally built the mansion for Ruby Keeler, Katie Sagal, and Charlie Sheen.

7. LONG-TIME HOME OF JOHN WAYNE, 4750 Louise Avenue

Wayne, a chain-smoker, lived here until he was stricken with lung cancer and decided to move to Newport Beach, where the air is easier to breathe. He lived here with his second wife, former call girl Esperanza "Chata" Bauer, and his third wife, Pilar Palette, from 1951 to 1965.

8. PHIL HARTMAN MURDER SITE, 5065 Encino Avenue

On May 28, 1998, actor Phil Hartman was murdered by his wife Brynn while he slept in the couple's bed. Brynn later committed suicide after police arrived and took custody of their two children. The 49-year-old comedian was best known for his roles on "Saturday Night Live" and the NBC sitcom "NewsRadio."

JUST OFF THE MAP, at 8424 Sepuleveda Ave., is the Palm Tree Inn, where "My Name is Earl" star Jason Lee and his TV brother (played by Ethan Suplee) supposedly live in the NBC comedy "My Name is Earl."

You can actually stay in the same room (231). However, you probably would not want to, given this is a high crime area. That part of town is known for its gang activity.

In the northwest part of the San Fernando Valley, are a few sites that are historic for reasons other than entertainment. The 6.7-on-the-Richter-scale January 17, 1994 earthquake which devastated Los Angeles had its epicenter in the community of Northridge. 16 of the 57 deaths occurred when the top floors of the Northridge Meadows Apartments at 9565 Reseda Boulevard collapsed on the bottom floor, killing tenants sleeping on the first level. The building has since been razed.

Also off the map is the site of the March 3, 1991, Rodney King beating incident, which occurred on a dirt field across from the Mountainback Apartments at 11777 Foothill Boulevard in Lakeview Terrace. It was the most publicized incident of police brutality in the nation. The April 28, 1992, acquittal of the four police officers who clubbed King 56 times led to the worst riots ever in the United States. (Two of the officers, Stacy Koon and Lawrence Powell, were subsequently convicted of federal charges.)

There are a few other movie and TV locations in the northern San Fernando Valley. The Ewing house featured on the "Dynasty" spin-off "Knots Landing" can be found on Crystalaire Place in Granada Hills. And at 11600 Eldridge Avenue in Lakeview Terrace, not far from the King beating site, is the former Lakeview Medical Center. The building would have been the Nancy Reagan Drug Center, but the residents of Lakeview Terrace, who objected to placing the center in their neighborhood, threatened to picket the Reagan Bel-Air mansion. Nancy withdrew her support for the project, and the building is now used exclusively for motion picture and television filming. Lakeview served as Pescadero State Hospital in *Terminator II* (1991)—the hospital where a crazed Linda Hamilton was imprisoned and the two Terminators had one of their many violent confrontations. The hospital was also seen as both hospitals in *Postcards from the Edge,* and was used for scenes in *Ricochet, Dying Young, Another 48 Hours, Heart Condition, She's Having a Baby,* and *Road House.*

In the western end of the Valley, Taft High School at 5461 Winnetka Ave. in Woodland Hills was transformed into West Dale High School for *The Brady Bunch Movie* (1995). Taft alumni include Lisa Kudrow, Maureen MacCormack, and Robin Yount.

OTHER CELEBRITIES WHO OWN HOMES IN THE SAN FERNANDO VALLEY: Sherman Oaks residents include Amy Brenneman, Albert Brooks, Gabrielle Carteris, Michael Chiklis, Ronnie Cox, Michael Dorn, Hector Elizondo, Gregory Harrison, James Earl Jones, David Leisure, Gavin MacLeod, Kristy McNichol, Pete Rose's ex-wife, Ryan Stiles, and Joe Walsh.

LeVar Burton, Jose Canseco, Dana Carvey, Tony Danza, William Devane, Patti Duke, Annette Funicello, Sara Gilbert, Macy Gray, David Hasselhoff, Melissa Manchester, Graham Nash, Edward James Olmos, Tom Petty, Tim and Daphne Reid, Ray Romano, Pat Sajak, Cybill Shepherd, Jean Smart, Patrick Swayze, Leslie Anne Warren, and Chuck Woolery own homes in Encino.

Kim Basinger, Vivica A. Fox, Nichele Nichols, and Barry van Dyke own homes in Woodland Hills. Tony Danza, Mo'Nique, and Nicholas Turturro live in Tarzana. Bruce Boxleitner and Melissa Gilbert, Brandy, Jada Pinkett and Will Smith live in Calabasas. When they were married, Nick Lachey and Jessica Simpson also owned a home in Calabasas prior to their divorce.

Charlie Sheen had his share of problems in his Agoura Hills home. Jamie Foxx owns a 10-bedroom home in the Thousand Oaks community of Hidden Valley. Other Valley homeowners include Lisa Bonet, Beau Bridges, John Davidson, Bob Eubanks, Ted Lange, Matt LeBlanc, Lisa Marie Presley, Mickey Rooney, Denise Richards, Jack Scalia, and the "queen of disco," Donna Summer.

When Steven Spielberg's locations scouts searched for a house to use as Elliott's in E.T., they looked for a typical suburban house that looked like it had a magical mountain and a redwood forest behind it. They found the house in the northwest section of the San Fernando Valley (7121 Lonzo Street, Tujunga), situated in front of one of the highest peaks of the San Gabriel Mountains. E.T. took up residence here after being stranded by his fellow travelers, and Elliott hid him until both were discovered by government agents. The Halloween street scenes and the chase scenes, though, were filmed on several different streets of Porter Ranch, another community in the northwestern portion of the San Fernando Valley. The famous scene in which Elliott and his friends, seemingly cornered by police cars, fly away into the air on their bicycles was filmed on White Oak Drive in Northridge, between Tribune and San Fernando Mission Roads.

Will Smith and Jada Pinkett live on a secluded 100 acre ranch located in the San Fernando Valley suburb of Calabasas. They purchased the property from singer Bobby Vinton. The property has its own lake.

OTHER POINTS OF INTEREST IN OR NEAR LOS ANGELES

• **"HOSTAGE" HOUSE,** 2960 Tuna Canyon Road, Topanga

This fortress-style home, situated high on a hill, was the seemingly impenetrable home of a Mob accountant in 2005's *Hostage*. Bruce Willis had to rescue the accountant's children from teenagers who took the kids hostage.

• **MALIBU CREEK STATE PARK,** Las Virgenes Road, Malibu

This park was once Century Ranch, a Twentieth Century Fox back lot. It was purchased by the State of California in 1974 and continues to be a frequent filming site. The park was where incoming choppers brought in the wounded in television's "M*A*S*H" (as well as in the 1970 movie of the same name). The park has also been the site of the first and at least one *Planet of the Apes* sequel, *Butch Cassidy and the Sundance Kid,* and *Tora! Tora! Tora!*

• **PARAMOUNT RANCH**, 1813 Cornell Road, Agoura (north of Malibu Creek State Park)

This national park was once owned by Paramount Studios. Still in existence is a "Western Town," which includes a general store, wood shop, barn and bridge used in the filming of "The Virginian," "Have Gun, Will Travel," "The Riflemen," "Bat Masterson," "Dr. Quinn, Medicine Woman," and dozens of other films and television series.

Free tours are given on an irregular basis. Call (818) 597-9192 for additional information.

• **SIX FLAGS MAGIC MOUNTAIN,** 26101 Magic Mountain Parkway, off Interstate 5, (805) 255-4111

The amusement park was turned into Wally World in *National Lampoon's Vacation* (1983). It has also doubled as Wisconsin Wonderland, the amusement park seen in the opening credits of the ABC sitcom "Step by Step," which starred Patrick Duffy and Suzanne Somers.

• **VASQUEZ ROCKS COUNTY PARK,** 10700 Escondido Canyon Road, Agua Dulce (northeast of Newhall on Route 14)

Fodors calls it "one of Los Angeles County's best photo opportunities [even though it's almost] a two-hour drive from downtown." The main attraction are the unusual angular rocks that one might expect to encounter on an alien planet. Dozens of Western and science fiction movies (including *Star Trek IV, Star Wars* and *Starship Troopers*), and television shows (the original "Star Trek") have been filmed there. The city of Bedrock in *The Flintstones* (1994) was also built by the rocks.

• **"NIGHTMARE ON ELM STREET" HOUSE,** 1428 N. Genesee Avenue, Hollywood

The two-story white house where Freddy Krueger ran amok is located in Hollywood, just south of Nichols Canyon.

• HOUSE AT 1530 ORANGE GROVE AVENUE, Hollywood

Jamie Lee Curtis lived here in *Halloween* (1978). The street, two blocks west of Genesee, is used frequently as a filming site because it does not have palm trees and looks midwestern.

• "MUSIC BOX" STAIRS, 900 block of Vendome Street, Silver Lake

In the Academy Award-winning 1932 film short *The Music Box*, Laurel and Hardy, playing bumbling piano delivery men, tried to move a piano up these stairs. The steps are located just south of Sunset Boulevard between Descanso Drive and Vendome Street.

• USC/COUNTY HOSPITAL, 1200 N. State Street, East Los Angeles

Featured as Port Charles Hospital in "General Hospital."

• WOMEN'S AND CHILDREN'S HOSPITAL, 1240 N. Mission Road, Boyle Heights

The hospital featured in the NBC sitcom "Scrubs."

• SHOOTING OF MARVIN GAYE, 2101 S. Gramercy Place

On April 1, 1984, the singer was shot to death by his father, Reverend Marvin Gaye, Sr., in Mid-City, a community south of Hancock Park.

• HUNTINGTON PARK HIGH SCHOOL, 6020 Miles Avenue, Huntington Park

Most of the scenes from the musical *Grease* (1978), starring John Travolta and Olivia Newton-John, filmed here, including the dance, the principal's office, the auto shop and the bleachers (although not the final carnival scene, which was filmed at John Marshall High, and the front exterior, which was filmed at Venice High School).

- **GARFIELD HIGH SCHOOL,** 5101 E. Sixth Street
  The movie *Stand and Deliver* (1988) was based on a true story about this East Los Angeles school. The students, underprivileged and expected to underperform, were taught to excel in calculus for a state test by a teacher, Jaime Escalante, who was portrayed in the movie by Edward James Olmos. When the students performed well above average, the state testing agency accused the students of cheating and invalidated the scores. Given the choice of either accepting the testing service's decision or retesting, the students chose to "stand and deliver."

- **PUENTE HILLS MALL,** Colima Road, Puente Hills
  In *Back to the Future* (1985), Christopher Lloyd was gunned down by terrorists, and Michael J. Fox took Lloyd's DeLorean back in time, in the parking lot of the J. C. Penney's at the mall.
  The high school featured was Whittier High School, 12417 Philadelphia Street, Whittier.

- **MONROVIA CITY HALL,** 415 S. Ivy, Monrovia
  Was transformed into the Rome, Wisconsin courthouse in the acclaimed CBS drama "Picket Fences." The police station was located next door at 140 East Lime. Tom Skerritt and Kathy Baker's house was at 211 North Highland.

• **THE UNITED METHODIST CHURCH,** 3205 "D" Street, La Verne
   The church featured in both *The Graduate* (1967) and *Wayne's World 2* (1992).

• **SHAMROCK MEATS,** 3461 E. Vernon Avenue (corner Alcoa Avenue), Vernon
   In the first *Rocky* (1976), Sylvester Stallone worked here and practiced for prize fights by punching slabs of beef. Scenes from *The Mambo Kings* (1992) were also shot here.

• **KERN'S OF CALIFORNIA,** 13010 East Temple Avenue, City of Industry
   In the first *Terminator* (1984), Arnold Schwarzenegger was crushed to death in this food manufacturing and canning facility.

• **VENICE HIGH SCHOOL,** 13000 Venice Boulevard, Venice
   One of the three high schools used as Rydell High School in *Grease* (1978). Also featured as Edward Furlong's high school in *American History* X (1988).

• **LOS ANGELES INTERNATIONAL AIRPORT**
   Airplane! (1980) is probably the most famous of the many movies filmed at LAX.

• **CAMERON DIAZ'S BEACH HOUSE IN "CHARLIE'S ANGELS,"** 2028 The Strand, Hermosa Beach
   In *Charlie's Angels II: Full Throttle* (2002), Diaz shared this home with Luke Wilson.

• **"BEVERLY HILLS 90210" BEACH HOUSE,** 3500 The Strand, Hermosa Beach

Tori Spelling, Brian Austin Green, and Jennie Garth lived in this beach house on "Beverly Hills 90210." The house was also Dan Aykroyd's house in *My Stepmother is an Alien* (1988) and Sissy Spacek's home in the horror film *Carrie* (1976).

• **PORTOFINO INN,** 260 Portofino Way, Redondo Beach

In *Cannonball Run* (1981), starring Burt Reynolds and dozens of other stars, the finish line of the cross-country speed car race was filmed extensively here. The hotel was also "Hotel Malibu" in the short-lived TV series of that name.

• **KING HARBOR**, Beryl Street, Redondo Beach

Setting of the NBC crime show "Riptide," which aired between 1984 and 1986.

• **TORRANCE HIGH SCHOOL,** 2200 West Carson Street, Torrance

The high school depicted as West Beverly High in the early years of "Beverly Hills 90210" and Sunnydale High in the television series "Buffy the Vampire Slayer." It was also Freddie Prinze, Jr. and Rachael Leigh Cook's high school in the teen flick *She's All That* (1999).

• **DEL AMO MALL**, 3 Del Amo Fashion Center, Torrance

The mall doubled as Phoenix's Saguro Square, where Billy Bob Thornton and Tony Cox worked, in 2003's black comedy *Bad Santa*.

It was also prominently featured in Quentin Tarantino's *Jackie Brown* (1997). As part of a plot to ensnare Samuel Jackson, Pam Grier supposedly exchanged clothes for money in Macy's women's department.

• **WAYFARER'S CHAPEL,** 5755 Palos Verdes Drive South, Rancho Palos Verdes

This unique glass-walled chapel, designed by Lloyd Wright, Frank Lloyd Wright's son, is a popular tourist attraction and is used frequently for movie wedding scenes, including Dennis Quaid and Meg Ryan's wedding in *Innerspace* (1987).

In real life "Beach Boy" Brian Wilson, Jayne Mansfield, Dennis Hopper, director Tom Shadyac, and "M*A*S*H" star Gary Burghoff were all married here.

• **PORTUGUESE POINT,** on Palos Verdes Drive South just south of the Abalone Cove parking lot

The buried treasure in *It's a Mad, Mad, Mad, Mad World* (1961), supposedly located under four palm trees at the fictitious Santa Rosita Beach State Park, was actually filmed on private property here. The filmmakers built their own park and brought in 70 sandango and palm fans.

• **QUEEN MARY,** Pier J at the end of Long Beach Freeway, Long Beach

The Queen Mary, one of the largest passenger liners ever built, has been in over 200 productions, most notably *The Poseidon Adventure* (1972). In *Someone to Watch Over Me* (1987), Mimi Rogers witnessed a murder in the swimming pool, which was transformed into a New York art museum (the producers put plexiglass over the pool).

The huge white geodesic dome next door, which once housed Howard Hughes' famous seaplane, the Spruce

Goose, has sometimes been rented to movie companies. The space station in *Stargate* (1994) and the Bat Cave and the Riddler's Lair in *Batman Forever* (1995) were built there.

• **"FERRIS BUELLER'S" HOME**, 4160 Country Club Drive, Long Beach

This private home appeared in the classic *Ferris Bueller's Day Off* (1986) starring Matthew Broderick.

• **LONG   BEACH   POLYTECHNICAL   HIGH SCHOOL,** 1600 Atlantic (at Pacific Coast Highway), Long Beach

Spike Jones and Cameron Diaz graduated from this high school, which was featured in *The Other Sister*, *American Pie I and II*, and *Coach Carter*

• **HYATT REGENCY HOTEL**, 200 S. Pine Avenue, Long Beach

The most entertaining action sequences in 1993's *Last Action Hero* were staged on the hotel's roof, where Arnold Schwarzenegger crashed a gangster's funeral, stole the corpse, and while dodging the mourners' gunfire, jumped onto an outdoor glass elevator (added especially for the movie), only to have to dodge artillery fire from a helicopter. Schwarzenegger shot out the helicopter, but the elevator collapsed, forcing him to make a midair grab onto the corpse. Schwarzengger fell again, this time into a specially created Hollywood version of the La Brea Tar Pits (a mulch made with Oreo cookie dye). Fortunately, Schwarzenegger's movie daughter (a young Bridgette Wilson) arrived just in time with a change of clothes.

- **VETERANS ADMINISTRATION MEDICAL CENTER**, 5901 E. Seventh Street (at Pacific Coast Highway), Long Beach

    The VA Hospital's facade is depicted as "Wilshire Memorial Hospital" in "Melrose Place."

- **SANTA ANA TRAIN STATION,** 1000 E. Santa Ana Boulevard, Santa Ana

    The place where Tom Cruise said goodbye to Dustin Hoffman in the final scene of *Rainman* (1988); and where Chevy Chase, accompanied by Darryl Hannah, eluded his pursuers in *Memoirs of an Invisible Man* (1992).

- **MAIN PLACE, SANTA ANA,** 2800 N. Main Street, Santa Ana

    The mall where Arnold Schwarzenegger arrested bad guy Richard Tyson in *Kindergarten Cop* (1990).

- **MEDIEVAL TIMES RESTAURANT**, 7662 Beach Boulevard, Buena Park

    In *The Cable Guy* (1996), Matthew Broderick defended himself from the violent assaults of his new friend, Jim Carrey.

- **HOAG HOSPITAL**, 301 Newport Avenue, Newport Beach

    The exterior was depicted as the Miami hospital in the NBC comedy "Empty Nest" and its spin-off "Nurses."

ACKNOWLEDGMENTS

There are so many people that I need to thank that it is difficult to know where to start. In researching this book, I interviewed or consulted with many location managers, operators of location services, publicists, librarians, realtors, and other entertainment industry professionals.

Perhaps it would be fitting to start with the members of the various city and state film commissions: Dirk Beving and his staff at the City of Los Angeles Film and Video Permit Office; Lisa Mosher, librarian; Hugh Cooper, permit coordinator, and Amy Gutierrez, intern at the California Film Commission; Jason Hartman of the Los Angeles County Film Office; Ariel Penn, film liaison, city of Pasadena; Benita Miller, special event coordinator of Beverly Hills' Department of Public Services; Ian Tanza of the West Hollywood Film Commission; Christopher Reed, the former permit coordinator of Culver City; Richard Wiles, who issues permits for the city of Vernon; and Cheryl Adams of the Santa Clarita Film Commission.

I would like to especially thank Diane Klein, Antoinette Levine, Robin Citrin, Donald Potts, Jack English, Joseph Luizzi, Sr., and the other location managers, location scouts and operators of location services who helped me: Ned Shapiro, Steve Dawson, David Israel, Louis Goldstein, Paul Pav, Richard Davis, Bud Aronson, Annette Gahret, Peter Juliano, Billie Jenkins, Marie Warren, Bruce Rush, Keith Kramer, Craig Pointes, Richard Rosenberg, Marvin Bernstein, Bob Craft, Amy Ness,

Rhonda Baer, Taman McCall, David Preston, Ken Campbell, Mike Alvarado, Ken Rosen, Rick Rosen, Steph Benseman, Rowland Kirks, Ed Jeffers, Eva Schroeder, Kris Wagner, and Janice Polley.

As well, Randy Young, past president of the Pacific Palisades Historical Society; Phyllis Lerner of the Beverly Hills Historical Society; Hope Keimon, Tonie Carnes and Laura Verlaque of the Pasadena Historical Society; Betsy Goldman of the Venice Historical Society; Linda Brady of the Culver City Historical Society; Julie Lugocerra, Sony Pictures' liaison with the community and author of a forthcoming book on Culver City; Louise Gabriel of the Santa Monica Historical Society; and Dorothy Price and Sid Adair of the Windsor Square-Hancock Park Historical Society, were all very generous with their time and provided very helpful information.

Thanks also to the librarians who helped me research various topics, including Lisa Mosher of the California Film Commission; the staff of the Center for Motion Picture Studies in Beverly Hills; Shirley Kennedy and her staff at the Academy of Television Arts and Sciences; the librarians at the Los Angeles Public Library, Pasadena Public Library, and the Orange County Public Library, particularly the El Toro branch; Raymond Soto, UCLA Film and Television Librarian; Jennie Watts, Julie Yamamoto, and Diane Lehoven of the Huntington Library; Ken Kenyon of 20th Century Fox; Alline Merchant of the Brand Library; Tim Gregory of the Pasadena Historical Society; and Robert Tieman, assistant archivist, Walt Disney Studios.

Gary Sherwin, former director of media relations, and Connie Eldridge of the Los Angeles Convention and Visitors Bureau, were most helpful; as were Jill Singer of the Donahue Group, which represents the Beverly Hills

Visitors Bureau, and Victoria King of the Hotel Bel-Air. A number of other public relations professionals gave generously of their time, including Andy Marx; Lindsey Jones; Saul Kahan; Michael Klastorin; Paul Gendreau; Chris Tomasko; Denise Greenawalt; Doug Taylor; Liz Gengl; Richard Neely; John West; Fred Howard; Jill Tsukatoma; Rich Bornstein; Georgianna Francisco; Tom Gray; Teri Bond Michael, Karen Mack, Mary Tokita and James Blaine of UCLA; Tom Witherspoon of the Queen Mary; Diane Barnhart of Caltech; Mary Blaze of Beverly Hills Hotel; Karen Wong of the Santa Monica Convention and Visitors Bureau; Harry Medved of the Screen Actors Guild; Kelly Greene of the Hollywood Roosevelt Hotel; Cliff Gallo of the American Film Institute; Kenlyn Elipsen of the Huntington; LuAnn Munns of Los Angeles State and County Arboretum; Barbara Leigh of the former St. James Club; Maureen Stokes of The Biltmore (and David Morgan, who oversees filming there); Jim Yeager, director of publicity, Universal Studios Hollywood; Mike Rosenberg of the Los Angeles Coliseum; Julie Taylor of the Pacific Design Center; Rick Stevens of the California Highway Patrol; and Jeff Bliss of Pepperdine.

And I certainly have not forgotten Marsha Meyer Sculatti of the West Hollywood Marketing Associaton; and Amy Anderson of the West Hollywood Convention & Visitors Bureau; Luc Tamarra of the Los Angeles Unified School District; Kari Johnson, curator of the Hollywood Studio Museum; Al Davis, general manager of the Magic Castle; Mrs. Jay (Ramona) Ward of Dudley Doo-Rite Emporium; Nicky Blair; Denise Carrejo of Damar; Dee Stanley, Walker Location Services; Kevin Beggs of the "Baywatch" production staff; Doug MacArthur, former manager of the Yamashiro; Judy Hunter, executive director of the Pasadena Historical Society; Don Zepfel, vice president, production, Universal Studios; Mary Fry, general manager and Beth Savage, executive assistant of Raleigh Studios; Lorraine Shaw, business affairs, and Richard Schnyder, vice president, sales, Hollywood Center Studios, business affairs; Debbie Ross, manager of the Montecito Apartments; Ana Martinez-Holler of the Hollywood Walk of Fame; Manny Weltman, whose passion for historical accuracy should be shared by more chroniclers of Hollywood history; Stephanie Pond-Smith of Carolco; Eileen Garcia, president of the South Pasadena Chamber of Commerce; Steve Rose, president of the Culver City Chamber of Commerce; Dee Powers, owner of the Port Cafe; Josh Avin and Jason Vance of the Hotel Mondrian; Randall Makinson, director and curator of the Gamble House; Timothy Buchanan, principal of Burroughs High School; Don Waldrop, president, Franklin Hills Residents Association; Raoul H. Pinno, film and photo shoot manager, UCLA; Patricia Cohen Samuels of Spago; Richard Terra, vice president, Shamrock Meats; Nelson Crispo, USC film coordinator; Steve Harris, manager of the Castle Green Apartments, Pasadena; Norma Tomkinson of the J. W. Marriott Hotel; Tom O'Brien, personnel director, Kern's of California; Jane Gilman, editor of the *Larchmont Chronicle*; Rick Rossini, assistant principal, Van Nuys High School; Tom Buckley, film coordinator of Union Station; Abel Ramirez, manager of Caltech's Atheneum; Susan Thompson of the Westin Bonaventure; Ruth Richards of the South Pasadena Preservation Society; Andy Stamatin of the Shrine Auditorium; Robin Faulk, marketing director, Santa Monica Place; Joe Walker, assistant principal, Grant High School; Bob Sirchia, vice president of Culver Studios; Ellen West and Ed Giles of the Department of Water and Power; Mark Stokhaug, director of security for 444 S. Flower Street; Richard Adkins, executive director, Hollywood

Studio Museum; Ruth Ryon and Steve Harvey of the Los
Angeles Times; Richard Taylor, head of fire and security,
Warner Hollywood Studios; Tracy Fowler of the Century
Plaza Hotel and Towers; Barbara Rosenman of Los Angeles
Parks and Recreation (Greystone); Joseph DiSante,
manager of guest services, ABC-TV; Stephanie DeWolf,
assistant planner, and Randy Shulman, planning intern, of
the Pasadena Urban Conservation Department; Officer
Chuck Foote, Los Angeles Police Academy; Sgt. Larry
Thompson, Los Angeles Police Department film
coordinator; Richard Munitz, assistant principal, Beverly
Hills High School; Marge Maple and Nancy O'Connor of
Hollywood Memorial Park Cemetery; Karen Sanders of the
Pasadena Convention and Visitors Bureau; Norma
LeValley, editor, *South Pasadena Review;* Charlie Morton,
former owner of the "Dynasty" house; Peter Pampush,
assistant director, student affairs, USC School of Cinema
and Television; Bob Bacon of Ramsey-Shilling Realtors;
Deborah Bieber and Denise Mathis of Bellefontaine
School; Sandra Griffin, property manager of the El Royale
Apartments; David Bowen of "Step by Step," Jodi
Hutchinson of Six Flags Magic Mountain; Judy Bijlani,
marketing director, Main Place, Santa Ana; Cecyle
Rexrode, Shirley Krims and David Horowitz of Warner
Bros.; Connie Humburger of LA Conservancy; Carolyn
Lucci of the Sherman Oaks Galleria; Paul Garcia, buildings
and grounds manager of the Wayfarers Chapel; Ellen Appel
Public Relations; Larry Paull; Emily Ferry; Marcia Reed
and Jim Bissel.

For helping me keep the book up to date, I would
like to thank Laura Meyers; Laurie Jacobson, the author of
Hollywood Haunted; Elaine Young and Jeff Hyland; Adam
Gooch of Southland Title; Rachel Smookler and Monica
Poling of the old Hollywood Entertainment Museum;

Marcia Tyselling of Star Wares; Erik Porter of the Malibu Film Office; Steve Lawler, project manager of filming at the Ambassador Hotel; Geri Pitt of the Four Seasons at Beverly Hills; Karen Millet of Victoria King Public Relations; Jill Perry of Caltech; Marlene Armas-Zermeno of the Biltmore Hotel; Lisa Baur of the Park Plaza Hotel; Pamela Bellew of Occidental College; Frank Cooper of the Art Deco Society; Kirk Slaughter of Castle Ivar; Sophie Lafferty of Castle Green; Tony Garcia, principal, Huntington Park High School; Ben Jacobs, principal, Venice High School; Nyla Arslanian; Carol Martinez and John Duel of the Los Angeles Convention & Visitors Bureau; Jeb Baird of the Beverly Hills Conference & Visitors Bureau; Dustin Scheerer; and Rick Schuler, Steve Millar, John P. Crumlish, Ralph Chaump, David Lamp, and Mick Lehr. Scott Carter took me on a memorable tour of movie sites of South Pasadena.

Jeff Huttner, author of *The LA Bargain Book*, and his assistant Linda Roberts; Kathryn Leigh Scott of Pomegranate Press; Julie von Zerneck and Joseph Naud of Portrait of a Bookstore; Stephanie Jones of the Automobile Club of Southern California; Karen Perea of Barnes & Noble; Steven Abrams; Paul Keane; Adele Pearlstein; Ronnie Silverstone; and Margaret Fishman all provided valuable advice which I appreciate.

And finally, I'd like to thank those involved in the production of this book, including my editor, Lisa Rojany, for her invaluable and painstaking editorial expertise; Matt Holcomb, Ron Fishman and Adam Fishman for their invaluable computer assistance; and Julian Wasser, who provided many of the photographs included here.

My apologies to anyone I inadvertently left out.

A NOTE ABOUT FUTURE EDITIONS

The Ultimate Hollywood Tour Book is updated annually, and future editions will include the latest filming locations, as well as updated listings and additional points of interest.

If you know of a filming location or other site not mentioned in this book—and if we use the information, subject, of course, to verification—we will send you a free copy of the next edition of the book.

Tips should be e-mailed to info@nrbooks.com or mailed to

North Ridge Books
P. O. Box 1463
Lake Forest, CA 92609

ABOUT THE AUTHOR

William A. Gordon is a full-time author and publisher whose other books include *Shot on This Site: A Traveler's Guide to the Places and Locations Used to Film Famous Movies and Television Shows.*

His acclaimed study of the May 4, 1970, killings at his alma mater, Kent State University, *Four Dead in Ohio: Was There a Conspiracy at Kent State?*, was praised by *Choice* magazine "as entertaining as the best detective fiction and as analytical and well documented as the best journalism or scholarship."

He is also the editor of *The Quotable Writer: Words of Wisdom from Mark Twain, Aristotle, Oscar Wilde, Robert Frost, Erica Jong, and More. Wilson Library Bulletin,* which reviewed an earlier version of the book, called it "irresistible" and wrote that "Gordon has succeeded in selecting the most memorable, thought-provoking, important, funny and/or outrageous quotations about the book world."

A native of Akron, Ohio, Mr. Gordon currently lives near Los Angeles.

INDEX

PHOTO CREDITS

Cover photos: Mann's Theater ©Donna Carroll; Universal Studios ©1994 Universal City Studios; Maps to the Stars' Homes ©Mark Wanamaker/Bison Archives.

All other photos are © William A. Gordon except as indicated:
Pages 23 (Beverly Hills Hotel), 32 (Manson murder site), 38 (Madonna and Brad Pitt homes), 43 (Ronald Reagan/"Beverly Hillbillies" houses), 49 (Spelling and Playboy Mansions), 68 (Roseanne, Marilyn Monroe), 75 (Arnold Schwarzenegger), 86 (Malibu Colony, Ungar/Carson estates), 89 (Broad Beach), 108 (Century City), 118 (Belushi van at the Chateau Marmont), 185 (former Nicholson home), 234 (Warner Bros.) © Julian Wasser.

Pages 83 (Halle Berry homes), Pgs. 120 (Johnny Depp and Cristina Aguilera), Pg. 183 (Denzel Washington and Eddie Murphy) ©Fame Pictures.

Pages 23 (Tom Cruise), Pg. 71 (Arnold Schwarzenegger), Pg. 53 (Chemosphere), Pg. 83 (Britney Spears) ©Celebrity Photos.

Page 64 (Regent Beverly Wilshire) courtesy Beverly Hills Visitors Bureau/©Martin Elkort. Page 64 (Gregg Donovan) courtesy Gregg Donovan. Page 75 (Thelma Todd Café) courtesy Randy Young/Pacific Palisades Historical Society. Page 95 (Santa Monica Pier) courtesy Santa Monica Convention and Visitors Bureau/Justine Hill. Page 108 (Marilyn Monroe crypt) ©Jill Adams, www.forevermarilyn.com.

Page 122 (Sunset Tower Hotel) courtesy West Hollywood Marketing Corporation/Tim McHugh; Page 152 (Mann's Chinese Theater) courtesy Cinamerica Theaters. Page 152 (Hollywood Walk of Fame) and 159 (Capitol Records) courtesy Los Angeles Convention and Visitors Bureau/©1991 Michele and Tom Grimm. Page 168 (Castle Ivar) courtesy Kurt Slaughter.

Page 198 (Griffith Park) and 211 (City Hall) courtesy Los Angeles Convention and Visitors Bureau/©1991 Michele and Tom Grimm. Page 207 (Westin Bonaventure Hotel) courtesy Westin

Bonaventure. Page 207 (Biltmore Hotel Olive Street entrance) courtesy Biltmore Hotel. Page 211 Shrine Auditorium, courtesy Shrine Auditorium & Exposition Center.

Page 222 (Gamble House) courtesy The Gamble House. Page 229 (Queen Anne cottage) courtesy Los Angeles State and County Arboretum. Page 238 (Universal Studios) ©1990 University City Studios.

A GREAT GIFT BOOK FOR WRITERS

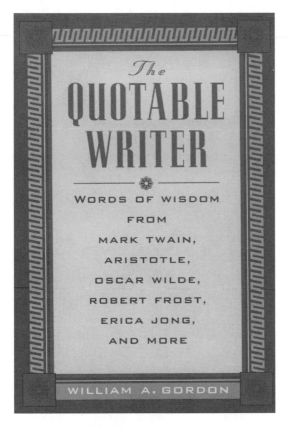

"William A. Gordon has created a Bartlett's of the literary life, culling and collecting roughly a thousand of the best things ever said or written by and about writers and writing."

—From the foreword by David A. Fryxell,
editorial director, *Writer's Digest*

Autographed copies are available for $14.95 plus $4.00 shipping and handling from North Ridge Books, P. O. Box 1463, Lake Forest, CA 92609. CA residents add $1.20 sales tax.

Additional information and sample quotes can be found at
www.nrbooks.com.

Additional copies of

THE ULTIMATE
HOLLYWOOD
TOUR BOOK

can also be ordered by sending $16.95 and
$4.00 shipping and handling to:

NORTH RIDGE BOOKS
P.O. BOX 1463
LAKE FOREST, CA 92609

California residents add $1.36 sales tax.

For overseas orders please add $12.00
for air mail shipping and handling.